# Dr. Chi

# LEARN TO READ
# BOOK

## FOR ALL AGES

A complete learn-to-read program
for <u>everyone</u>!!

✓ **For home schoolers**
✓ **For teachers**
✓ **For adult literacy programs**
✓ **For anyone who wants to**
   **teach someone to read**

# Dr Christman's Learn-to-Read Book

Published by:

**BLUE BIRD PUBLISHING**
**2266 S. Dobson #275**
**Mesa AZ 85202**
**(602) 831-6063**
**FAX (602) 831-1829**
**E-mail: bluebird@bluebird1.com**
**Web site: http://www.bluebird1.com**

ISBN 0-933025-17-3
$15.95

Illustrations by Catharine Christman

**Library of Congress Cataloguing-in-Publication Data**

Christman, Ernest H.
    [Learn to read book for all ages]
    Dr. Christman's learn to read book for all ages: a complete learn-
    to-read program for everyone, for home schoolers, for teachers, for
    adult literacy programs, for anyone that wants to teach someone to
    read.

        p.      cm.
    ISBN 0-933025-17-3   :     $15.95
       1. Reading (Elementary)--Phonetic method. 2. Readers    I. Title:
    Learn to read book for all ages.
    LB1573.3C47       1990
    372.4'145--dc20                    90-33029
                                              CIP

# About the Author

Ernest H. Christman is a graduate of the University of Pennsylvania School of Medicine. He completed his specialty training in ophthamology at the Massachusetts Eye and Ear Infirmary in Boston. Currently in private practice, he has held academic appointments at Harvard University, Temple University, and the University of Pennsylvania. He is the author of numerous research papers and books. An avid linguist, he researched reading difficulties in English and other languages. This book, a new approach to learning to read, is the result.

# About the Illustrator

Catharine Ann Christman Barber is a graduate of the University of New Mexico (music performance) and the University of Notre Dame School of Law. She is a trial attorney for the United States Department of Justice in Washington D.C. The illustrations were first done when she was fouteen, in an endeavor to stimulate her younger brother to read.

---

**DR. CHRISTMAN'S DEDICATION**
Dedicated to my son, Earnest Daniel Christman,
who caused this book to be written.

---

## TABLE OF CONTENTS

## INTRODUCTION

Reading is simply the "sounding out" of letters and letter combinations according to the rules of English. What we understand in our minds is the sounds, not the symbols. Symbols represent the sounds.

Blind people communicate verbally as well as sighted persons, but they read using Braille, a tactile symbol system. It must be emphasized that symbols work only when the viewer has a memory of their meaning. This also applies to cultural symbols such as male-female figures on restroom doors, traffic signs, and religious emblems.

In order to learn reading, all that is needed is a system. This book uses a progressive phonics system developed by Dr. Ernest Christman. After the alphabet is learned, then combinations of letters can be read as simple words. Progressively, more complicated letter combinations teach more complex sounds. Rather than teach just isolated words, sentences are incorporated from the very beginning to encourage good reading habits.

It is important that the student proceed from left to right in both words and sentences. Letting the eyes wander back and forth over words is the basis of reversals such as "saw" for "was."

A unique feature of this learn-to-read program is the stories at the end of each level. These stories are computer-checked to ensure that all the words comply with the phonic rules previously studied. Vocabulary is controlled on a phonic basis, not by a "look-say" word list. The students gets into actual reading quickly to encourage further study.

After studying the five levels in this book, the student will be able to "sound out" anything in written English and will have knowledge of phonic rules and syllabification.

## THE ALPHABET

It is absolutely necessary that the person beginning to read first know the alphabet, both large and small case.  The type used in this book:

A a  B b  C c  D d  E e

F f  G g  H h  I i  J j

K k  L l  M m  N n  O o

P p  Q q  R r  S s

T t  U u  V v  W w

X x  Y y  Z z

## LEVEL ONE

## THE SHORT *A* SOUND

Vowels have short and long sounds. When one says the letters of the alphabet, the names of the vowels are in the long vowel form. The short vowel sound, however, is more commonly encountered. It is usually found in the middle of a syllable.

Please read the large-type words with the student and point out that the letter *a* by itself is a long sound, the letter *a* in the word *at* has the short sound, and the addition of different letters before *at* changes the meaning of the word.

# a

# at

# rat

# hat

rat

hat

A fat rat sat on a hat.

A bat did nap on a mat.

Review and practice words with the *at* sound:

bat  fat  mat  hat
pat  rat  sat  vat

More practice words with the *short a* sound:

dad  sad  had
fad  lad  pad

map  rap  gap  lap
sap  tap  nap  zap

ham  bam  jam
ram  Pam  Sam

More practice words with the *short a* sound:

rag   hag   bag   gag
lag   nag   tag   wag

man   ban   Dan   fan
pan   ran   tan   van

Dad had a map in a tan van.

More practice words with the *short a* sound:

fat tan van map
rat nap gas tab
fan pad dad bag
man sad ham dam

Sam sat on the lap of the sad man.*

* The *the* sound will be explained on page 63.

More practice words with the *short a* sound:

fan   had   wag   gag
lad   jam   rag   tan

Dan   Pam   Sam   gap
fad   pass   pan   ran

Sam had ham and jam in a pan.

# THE LONG *A* SOUND

The addition of a second vowel to a syllable is a device that tells the reader to lengthen the sound of the first vowel. A syllable <u>by definition</u> can have only one vowel sound. **The added vowel is silent, it is never sounded.**

The most common example is the addition of the "silent e" at the end of a syllable. This vowel is only a guide to pronunciation and is not to be sounded.

The teacher should read the following word pairs with the student so he can hear the lengthening of the vowel. The student then reads them to the teacher.

fat fate    hat hate    rat rate

fad fade    mad made    tap tape

gap gape    Dan Dane    pan pane

Sam same    cap cape    mat mate

man mane    pal pale

nap nape    at ate

Practice words with the *long a* sound:

late   pave   tame   sake

safe   name   save   wade

gale   ate   wave   Dave

rake   lake   gaze   gate

lame   fake   vane   ape

sale   take   mane   wake

made   Jane   mate   lame

same   gape   sake   safe

Some practice sentences with the *long a* sound:

The tame ape gave a wave to Dave.

Kate did hate to take the rake to the gate.

Jane did bake a cake to take to the sale.

More practice words with the *long a* sound:

Kate game bake lame

pane haze tape fade

fate wave make male

late hate pave tame

vase same sane tale

lane sale wake dame

date fake gale gate

daze gaze gape fame

## THE *SHORT I* SOUND

The same rules for pronouncing *letter a* apply for *letter i*. *Letter i* is pronounced short when it is in the middle of a syllable.

bib fib rib bid

hid lid kid rid

did big dig jig

pig rig him Jim

Kim Tim rim dim

Bill pill Jill kill

fill hill kiss miss

Some more practice words with the *short i* sound:

bin  pin  sin  tin

win  lip  nip  rip

sip  tip  zip  bit

fit  hit  kit  lit

sit  nit  pit  dip

bid  bin  his  hip

kid  rib  win  wit

Some practice sentences with the *short i* sound

Jim had a fit and bit his lip.

The pin in the kit did not fit.
It made a rip in it.

A big pig did a jig on a tin bin.

## THE *LONG I* SOUND

A syllable can contain only one vowel sound. A "silent e" at the end of a syllable lengthens the *short i* sound into the *long i* sound.

hid hide    pin pine

bit bite    sit site

Tim time    bid bide

dim dime    kit kite

win wine    pip pipe

rip ripe    din dine

Some practice words with the *long i* sound:

dime lime ripe pipe bile

wipe dive hive jive dine

live site bite kite file

mite hike Mike pike hide

ride tide life wife fine

rite like nine vile dike

bike hive line mile lime

lite side pile time wide

Some practice sentences with the *short* and *long i* sounds.

# Tim had time to ride his bike to the dike.

# Mike had a kit to make a fine kite.

## The wife did not like to sit at the site of the big pine.

## THE *SHORT O* SOUND

The same rule applies to the vowel *o* as it did to the vowels *a* and *i*. Some *short o* sounds:

Bob  gob  lob  job

mob  sob  rob  God

hod  pod  rod  sod

Tod  nod  sog  bog

fog  hog  jog  log

box  Don  won  dot

got  fox  hop  hot

Some additional *short o* sounds:

tog  bop  hop  mop

pop  sop  top  dot

got  hot  jot  lot

not  pot  rot  tot

Don  Ron  mom  Tom

Bob  sod  hod  nod

sob  rob  pod  rod

box  pox  fox  Tod

Some sentences with the *short o* sound:

Tod had a job to mop the top of the pot.

Don did nod to Tom to hop on top of the sod.

It had not got hot, so Bob did jog on a log.

## THE *LONG O* SOUND

The addition of the "silent e" to a syllable containing an *o* causes the short sound to change into the long sound.

hop hope   rob robe
tot tote   rod rode   not note

Some practice words with the *long o* sound:

dope hope mope pope coke
rope dote rote tote woke
vote bone tone lone joke
home tome dome hole poke

mole pole role sole
lope node lode nose

Some practice sentences with the *long o* sound:

I hope to tote home the pole and rope.

I vote to put the bone in the hole as a joke
on the mole.

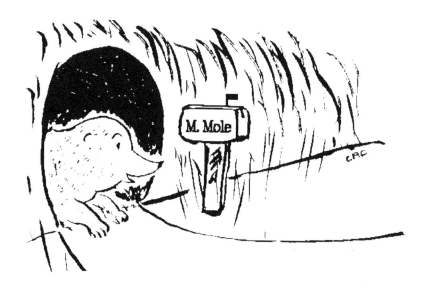

A mole has a hole for a home.

## THE *SHORT U* SOUND

The vowel *u* follows the same rules as for the other vowels. Some words with the *short u* sound:

hub  pub  rub  tub

bud  dud  mud  sud

bug  dug  hug  jug

lug  mug  rug  fuss

bum  gum  tug  muss

bun  dub  sub  fun

gun  pun  nun  nut

More words with *short u* sounds:

hum rum sum bun

fun gun nun pun

run sun but butt

hut rut bus putt

pus nut bug mutt

rub hug tub sub

muss fuss bull full

muff puff fuzz buzz

Some sentences with the *short u* sound:

Cut the fuss and run to the bus.

A bug dug a rut in the mud of the hut.

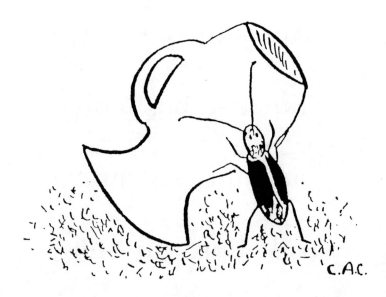

A bug did lug the jug on the rug.

## THE *LONG U* SOUND

The *vowel u* gets its long sound by the addition of a "silent e" to the same syllable.

tub tube   cut cute
dud dude   mutt mute

Some words with the *long u* sound:

tune  dune  fume  nude

rude  dude  tube  lube

mule  rule  mute  lute

duke  Luke  fuse  ruse

rube  fuze  dupe  June

Some sentences with the *long u* sound:

June did use the tube in the tub.

Luke did use the fuse as a ruse.

As a rule, a mule is rude to a dude.

## THE *SHORT E* SOUND

The *short e* sound follows the same rules as do the other four vowels. Some words with the *short e* sound:

den   hen   pen   ten

Ben   men   bet   jet

let   met   net   pet

set   wet   mess

yet   bed   led   Ned

red   Ted   wed   beg

peg   keg   leg   Meg

Some sentences with the *short e* sound:

Tess let a wet pet in the bed.

Ted led the ten men to the red keg.

The red hen set in a net in a pen.

## THE *LONG E* SOUND

In this combination, the "silent e" is placed next to the other *e*.

fed feed   bet beet   ten teen

pep peep   red reed   wed weed

Ned need   met meet   ten teem

Ken keen   fell feel

The letter *e* at the end of a syllable is usually pronounced long:

he   she   be   we   me

Some practice words with the *long e* sound:

peel feel heel keel

reel feet beet meet

feed seed deed heed

need reed weed seen

teen beef beep weep

deep keep peep seep

deem keen week seek

meek teem veer deer

Some sentences with *e* sounds:

Ned had no need to peep at the seed
on his feet.

I feel no need to feed the seed to a pet.

## THE LETTER Y

The vowels of the alphabet are *a*, *e*, *i*, *o*, and *u*. Letter *y* can function as both a vowel and a consonant.

Letter *y* functions as a consonant if it begins the word or syllable:

## yes yap yet

## yam yell yule

*Y* functions as a vowel if it is the only vowel in the syllable.

## gym myth gyp

If there is a "silent e" at the end of the syllable, the *y* in the syllable is pronounced long:

## byte hype type

## lyse pyre style

If letter *y* is at the end of the syllable, it is usually pronounced long:

fly   sky   shy   dry

why   spy   sly   try

wry   thy   sty   by

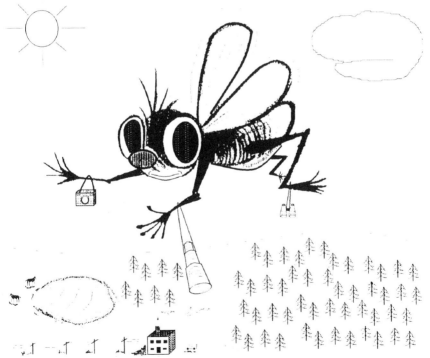

A shy fly did try to spy from the sky.

# THE CONSONANTS OF THE ALPHABET

## THE LETTER *K*

Letter *k* always represents a single sound:

kiss   keep   keel

keg   kit   kid

kite   kill   keen

Ken   Kim   kin

A practice sentence with the *k* sound:

Ken did keep his kite in a keg.

## THE LETTER *C*

Letter *c* has the *k* sound before the "hard" vowels *a, u,* and *o.*

Can   cat   cap

cab   cub   cuff

cut   cup   cop

cod   cob   cot

Some sentences with the *k* sound of letter *c*.

A cop had a cut in his cap.

A cat can nap on a cot.

## THE *CK* SOUND

This double consonant has the same sound as letter *k* alone:

rack    tack    sack

back    lack    hack

pock    pack    lock

rock    dock    sock

cock    hock    neck

mock    pick    muck

Dick    hock    heck

A practice sentence with the *ck* sound:

A duck did peck a sick cat on the neck.

More practice words with the *ck* sound:

tick    kick    sick

lick    neck    hick

peck    wick    buck

luck    duck    muck

suck    tuck    puck

deck    heck    rack

More sentences with the *ck* sound:

# Dick did lock the sock in a sack.

# Nick did tuck a duck in a pack on his back.

## THE HARD SOUND OF LETTER *S*

Letter *s* is often pronounced "hard" and sounds like letter *z*:

pills runs buns puns

guns beds tubs wigs

bills pens pigs tens

dens hens bugs fins

sells pins sins bins

ribs bibs tugs rugs

suds pads lids beds

More hard sounds of letter *s*. Note that when the preceding consonant is made with the vocal cords, the *s* takes on the voiced sound, pronounced like letter *z*:

tells  figs  buns  fibs

digs  dogs  fogs  mugs

kills  hums  sums  gums

bums  puns  hogs  jogs

hills  wells  logs  wins

hugs  jugs  bells  lugs

fans  fins  guns  puns

lens  tens  tons  pins

Some sentences with the hard *z* sound of letter *s*:

## The kids tell fibs to sell bells.

## The dog digs in the hills and finds bugs in logs.

## The hen kills bugs in the pens of the pigs.

# THE SOFT SOUND OF LETTER *S*

The following words demonstrate the soft sound of letter *s* that is heard after the unvoiced consonants *f, k, p,* and *t*. Unvoiced consonants are made without vibrating the vocal cords.

nests   mats   rests   bats

jumps   facts   rips   dots

lips   masks   maps   huts

pumps   huffs   sacks   pets

pups   tops   tips   locks

sips   hips   rats   pots

A sentence with the soft sound of letter *s:*

# The dog hops and jumps so fast that he huffs and puffs.

More practice words with the soft sound of letter *s*:

dusts    tops    cuffs

racks    bucks    hops

tips    lumps    hats

humps    ducks    bumps

asks    cops    puffs

keeps    weeps    seeps

A sentence with the soft sound of letter *s*:

The cat sleeps on the tops of the hats. He makes lumps and bumps on them.

## THE DIGRAPH

A digraph is a sound formed by combining two consonants to form a new sound *unlike* that of each of the letters.

The *CH* digraph is a hissing sound:

chip   chase   chum   chump

chill   chunk   chest   chose

chick   chop   check   chore

chap   chess   choke

cheek   chime   cheese

chat   chug   chin

More practice with the *ch* sound. Note that it can occur at both the beginning and at the end of the word:

| | | |
|---|---|---|
| **much** | **punch** | **chat** |
| **pinch** | **lunch** | **hunch** |
| **ranch** | **rich** | **bunch** |
| **chin** | **bench** | **chimp** |
| **champ** | **munch** | **belch** |
| **chide** | **chose** | **chums** |
| **beech** | **beach** | **finch** |

When the *ch* follows a vowel, letter *t* is often present to indicate that the vowel is pronounced short:

hatch   catch   match

batch   patch   notch

ditch   hitch   witch

fetch   botch   latch

itch   pitch   etch

In these and similar words, the *t* may or may not be pronounced at the speaker's option. Both pronunciations are equally correct and will be understood.

Some practice sentences containing the *ch* sound:

A bunch of rich chaps had lunch at the ranch.

A batch of chicks did hatch in that patch in the ditch.

The witch did fetch that chest with much punch in it.

# THE *SH* DIGRAPH

The *sh* digraph is found at both the beginning and at the end of a word:

shine   she   shin

shut   hash   push

sheep   shot   shell

shy   ship   bush

shop   bash   shape

dash   sheet   gash

Additional practice words with the *sh* sound:

shame   ash   wish

hush   lash   dish

shock   rash   shore

cash   shake   mash

fish   rush   short

sash   shave   sham

Some practice sentences with the *sh* sound:

She did push the sash of the shop shut.

The ship came to shore to sell fish for cash.

## THE *TH* DIGRAPH

The *th* sound may be a soft sound that is made without using the vocal cords. It can occur at the beginning or at the end of a syllable.

three    thin    theme    thick

moth    thug    length    thank

smith    math    cloth    broth

thud    with    worth    path

thud    thump    Ruth    bath

teeth    both    myth    month

fifth    sixth    width    north

The *th* can also be a hard, voiced sound at the beginning of a word:

| | | |
|---|---|---|
| **this** | **these** | **that** |
| **those** | **them** | **thy** |
| **then** | **thus** | **than** |
| **thee** | **thine** | **there** |

To tell when to use the hard of soft sounds of *th*, try it both ways. One way will be a meaningful sound (a word) while the other way will be a meaningless sound (not a word).

The word <u>the</u> can be pronounced two ways:

① <u>The</u> with a *long e* sound when the following word begins with a vowel.

② <u>The</u> with an *uh* sound when the following word begins with a consonant.

Practice with the student:

The end

The bike

A few practice sentences with the *th* sound:

# Those kids did thank these men for the thick broth.

## This thick cloth cape with the long length is worth three of those thin, short capes.

## THE *WH* DIGRAPH

The *wh* digraph is sounded with the vocal cords.  It occurs at the beginning of a word.

whip     whack     whim

whiff     whisk     whale

why     what     wham

wheel     when     while

whine     white     whit

whiz     whine     whey

Whig     which

A practice sentence with the *wh* sound:

The whip made a whack and a wham when it struck the white wheel.

## THE *NG* DIGRAPH

The *ng* is always sounded with the vocal cords and occurs at the end of a syllable:

sing    sang    song    bang

gang    rung    hung    lung

sung    fang    hang    rang

king    ring    wing    gong

dung    lung    ding    bong

ping    pong    Hong    Kong

Some sentences with the *ng* sound:

# The gang did sing a song while the bells rang.

## The king hung his ring on the ping-pong net.

## CONSONANT CLUSTERS

Consonant clusters are letters that, when sounded out in succession, almost blend into a new sound. This is different from a digraph that is a <u>new</u> sound formed by two letters.

The *ST* Cluster:

stud    store    steep

stove    stuck    stone

stem    stiff    still

strap    sting    stub

step    stick

storm    stank

Additional practice words with the *st* cluster:

stuff   stop   stink   staff

stag   stack   stand   stab

stun   stem   sty   stamp

stud   stub   stake   stall

stale   steed   steel   state

stash   stock   stint   stoke

stove   stunk   stomp   stuck

Some practice sentences with the *st* sound:

Stan had a stiff stick.  He struck the still
stone with it.

The kids had a hut with steep steps.

The *st* is one of the few consonant clusters found at both the beginning and at the end of words. Some *st* endings:

cast   fast   last   mast

vast   dust   lust   bust

rust   best   rest   test

list   mist   fist   jest

nest   gust   just   past

pest   vest   lest   chest

must   zest   west   midst

Some sentences with the *st* cluster:

The best stove must cost the most.  It must not rust like the rest.

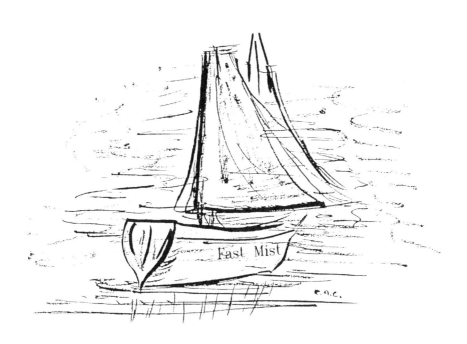

Fast Mist

The fast ship was lost in the mist.

## THE *NT* CLUSTER

The *nt* cluster is found only at the end of a word:

rent   lent   tent

dent   bent   sent

went   hint   lint

mint   tint   pant

rant   bunt   hunt

punt   runt   want

Some sentences with the *nt* sound:

I sent him the rent and he lent it to Kent.

The man went in the tent with the bent pole.

## THE *ND* CLUSTER

The *nd* cluster is found at the end of a word:

band    hand    land    sand

end    bend    lend    send

tend    bond    fond    pond

and    fund    mend    wind

fend    wand

stand    rend

Some practice sentences with the *nd* sound:

The men in the band have rents in the ends of the pants.  Let us lend them the funds to mend the rents.

I am fond of the sand on the land by the pond.

## VOWELS AND THE LETTER *R*

When a vowel is followed by *letter r*, the sound of the vowel is modified. Because *vowel o* is the strongest vowel, it is modified the least.

The *OR* Sound:

| | | | |
|---|---|---|---|
| cord | pork | porch | or |
| born | fort | corn | ford |
| lord | storm | for | bore |
| torn | fork | tore | form |

More practice words with the *or* sound:

cork    worn    stork    gore

sort    north    port    horn

torch    torn    store    dorm

short    more    fort    fork

lore    morn    worn    tort

tore    pore    sore    torn

Some practice sentences with the *or* sound:

# The short cord was worn and torn.

# The storm tore a hole in the north porch.

## THE *ER* SOUND

*Vowel e* is a weaker vowel and therefore is more affected by the following letter *r*.

herd    fern    terse

Bert    nerve    jerk

verse    berg    perk

berth    term    perch

herb    serve    her

nerd    germ    verb

Some sentences with the *er* sound:

## Bert did serve the herbs to her.

## He had the nerve to perch on her berth.

# MISCELLANEOUS

Here are some unusual phonic words to be learned now and explained in a higher phonic level.

Usually, vowels at the end of a syllable are pronounced long as in:

## go  so

Sometimes common words violate this rule, as in:

## to  do

Please note the words:

## of  off

The word off has no change in the sound value of the f. But when the stress falls on the f, as in the word of, it takes on the hard, voiced counterpart and is pronounced like letter v.

These miscellaneous words are introduced to make it easier to write Level One stories. The student should be able to read the following two stories without encountering anything not previously explained. It is recommended that the student first read these stories alone and then read them to the teacher. If any difficulties are encountered, the appropriate sections in this phonic level should be reviewed.

The student has now completed **Level One** of the **PROGRESSIVE PHONICS** reading method. The teacher should insist on good reading habits. The eyes must always go from left to right and decoding occurs as letter combinations are encountered and recognized. There should never be back-and-forth eye movement. This will slow the pace of reading and can cause reversals, such as interpreting *dog* for *god* and *was* for *saw*.

**Level Two** introduces more advanced phonic rules. The student should now appreciate that English is governed by a logic and that reading is not difficult if approached with an organized method.

# The Lake

Tom sat in the shade of the big bush by the side of the lake.  His dog went to run on the hot sand.  The dog's name is spot.  Tom did not chase him.  The sun had made the sand hot, and Tom had bare feet.  He did not feel like he had the pep to run.  So, Tom got a stick and gave it a toss for Spot to chase and bring back to him.  Spot did like this game, and when he got the stick he bit it and went back to Tom with it.  Tom gave the stick a huge toss to made it go far off.  Spot got it and came back with it.  Spot did not seem to tire of this game.

Jan had seen Tom and Spot and came by to talk.  She had her cat in her arms.  The cat had short legs and did not like to run in the hot sand.  Jan sat by Tom and put her cat in her lap.  Just then Spot came back with the stick.  The cat did not like the dog and ran to go home.  The dog gave chase.  The cat was not so fast, as his legs sank deep in the sand.  Spot did not need but a short time to catch up.  Tom did not think that Spot was a bad kind of a dog, that type of dog that bit cats.  Jan was not so sure that her cat was safe from harm.  She put a stone in her hand to toss at Spot in case he did jump on her cat.

Jan had no need to fret.  For Spot, it was the chase that was fun.  When he got close to the cat, he did not go as fast.  He did not want to catch the cat, but just make the cat run fast so it was more sport.

Jan did not like it that Spot made her cat run so fast. She got mad at Spot.

The cat ran to the shore of the lake and had to stop or get wet. He did not want to just sit still and let the dog catch him. But by luck the cat did see that a log was just off the shore. Jan did yell to her cat to jump on the log and get safe. The cat made a huge jump and got on the log. The dog came to a stop and just sat on the sand to watch the cat. Spot did not want to go on with the chase. It was hot. He sat on the shore and was glad to just watch the cat sit on the log.

Jan was mad at Spot for that hot chase on the sand. She had that stone in her hand and was set to toss it at Spot. She did not want to hit Spot, just to chase him off. Spot was a big dog and she did not want him to get mad and bite her. Tom went to Jan and got her to drop that rock. He told her that Spot was a tame dog and did not bite kids or cats. Her cat was safe. Spot did that chase for the fun of it, not to harm the cat. Just then Spot came to her and put his wet nose on her leg. He did want her to pet him. This she did. She was not mad at Spot for long.

Jan made a wave of her hand to get her cat to jump back from that log to the sand. But the cat did not seem to have the pep to make such a jump. The chase on the hot sand did tire him. He just sat on the log. It is a fact that cats hate to get wet. Jan's cat did not want to try that big jump, for that gap from log to shore did seem a bit wide. If he came up short, it was wet fur for him.

Tom had bare feet and did not care if he got them wet. It was just five steps from the shore to that log. Tom got the cat. As he went back to the shore, his heel struck a big thing that was stuck in the mud. It was so big that both feet did not feel the end of it. He gave the cat to Jan and went back to see what it was. He got a stick and made use of it to move some of the sand. It was a big chest.

Jan ran to her home to tell her mom and dad. She went by Tom's home to tell his mom and dad. All came to see what was in that chest in the sand. The men dug the chest free of the mud and sand. Then both of them did the hard task which was to lift and pull and drag that chest to the shore. The lock had so much rust on it that it just fell off. Then the kids got to lift the lid to see what was in the chest.

It was full of pots and pans and things like that. The chest had been in the mud for a long time. Most of the pots and pans had rust on them. On the side of the chest was the name of the ship that had sunk in the lake in a bad storm when Tom's dad was a small kid. That was a long time in the past. The kid that finds stuff like this may keep it.

Tom did feel that Jan and her cat made him find that prize. So, he will share the stuff in the chest with her. Jan got a dish pan and a brush. It was not hard to get the pots and pans to shine. Jan did want her mom to take her share of the pots and pans. But Jan's mom did not need more pots or pans. It was the same with Tom's mom.

Then Tom and Jan went to the store with the chest and all that stuff in it. The man at the store gave them cash for it. Then the kids spent a bit of the funds for bikes and games, and put the rest in the bank. It was fun to act rich for a short while.

Jan was glad that Spot had made up that game of chase her cat. She got to like him and did pet him when he went with Tom to her home. The kids went to walk by the shore at least six times a week to see if more free prizes did wash up on the sand. It had been luck to find that chest. It had been a big ship that sank, and more stuff is in the lake. Tom has a plan to find more things from that sunk ship. He will save up to get funds for the type of stuff that will let him probe deep in the sand and mud at the rim of the lake. His plan is to snag a box full of things and then bring his catch in to shore with a rope. He hopes to sell things from sunk ships for cash and get rich. Jan is not as apt to do this with him. The cost of the odds and ends Tom will need is not worth the price of a chest full of pots and pans, if he has the luck to find more stuff that is not junk. Tom will plan this for a week or so, and then feel it is not worth the fuss. Things will then get back to the norm in which Tom and Jan will run on the shore with his dog and her cat. The kids will not feel the need to probe all the big bumps in the sand in the hope to find a prize. Most of the time that is not wise, as the kids just get full of dirt and do not find a thing. The kids had a nice share of luck which is rare, and it is fun to tell that tale to pals.

# LEVEL TWO

## CONSONANT BLENDS

Consonant blends are consonant sounds that follow each other and blend slightly, but each sound (letter) is heard.

Note how the placement of letter *b* before letter *l* forms the *bl* consonant blend. Please read with the student:

lack <u>bl</u>ack   lend <u>bl</u>end

lock <u>bl</u>ock   less <u>bl</u>ess

Practice with consonant blends that occur at the beginning of words:

**br**:  rat brat      ring bring
      rag brag      rave brave

**cl**:  lip clip      lamp clamp
      lap clap      lump clump

**cr**:  rust crust     rest crest
      rash crash     rate crate

**dr**:  rug drug      rip   drip
      rag drag      rank drank

**fl**:  lock flock     lash flash
      lag  flag      lake flake

**fr**: rock frock    rank Frank
     red   Fred    risk   frisk

**gl**: lint glint    lobe globe
     loss gloss    land gland

**gr**: rip grip    race grace
     rim grim    raze graze

**pl**: lace place    lot   plot
     lug   plug    lane plane

**pr**: rank prank    rim prim
     robe probe    ride pride

E.T. did ride with pride his plane by the lane.

**sc**: cat scat     cab scab
      can scan    care scare

Scat, cat!

**scr**: roll scroll    rap scrap
      ram scram   rub scrub

**str**: rap strap    ride stride
      ring string   rip strip

**sk**: kid skid    kin skin
     kit skit     kill skill

**sl**: lip slip    lap slap
     lot slot    lack slack

**sm**: mall small    mile smile
     mug smug    mash smash

**sn**: nap snap    nip snip
     nob snob    nag snag

**sp**: pit spit    pill spill
     pot spot    pace space

**st**: top stop    tick stick
     tall stall    tore store

**sw**: well swell    weep sweep
     wing swing    wore swore

**tr**: rust trust    rap trap
     rip trip    rash trash

**tw**: wine twine    win twin
     wig twig    weed tweed

The twins did win wine and twine.

Consonant blends often occur at the end of words:

**ct**:   act    fact    tact    duct    pact

**ft**:   left    lift    raft    gift    soft

**ld**:   held    meld    gild    weld    bald

**lf**:   elf    self    golf    gulf    wolf

**lk**: milk   silk   sulk   bulk
      hulk   balk   talk   folk

**lm**: elm   film   helm   calm
      alm   balm   palm   whelm

**lp**: help   gulp   pulp   yelp
      alp   whelp   kelp   scalp

**lt**: belt   felt   melt   pelt
      hilt   jilt   silt   bolt

**mp**: camp   bump   jump   limp
      pump   ramp   lump   romp

**nd**: and   band   hand   end
      tend   mend   fund   pond

**nk**: bank   sink   ink   sank
      sunk   wink   bunk   link

**nt**: tent   bent   hint   dent
      sent   tint   rent   hunt

**pt**:  apt    kept    wept    rapt
crept    slept    opt    tempt

**sk**:  ask    risk    desk    task
mask    dusk    tusk    husk

**sp**:  asp    lisp    gasp    rasp
cusp    wasp    wisp    clasp

**st**:  must    fast    west    rust
nest    pest    vast    list

"It did sink,
It sank,
It had sunk.

We will see it
no more."

## SYLLABLE DIVISION

A syllable is a word, or part of a larger word, that is pronounced with a single, uninterrupted sounding of the voice. A syllable must contain **only one** vowel sound. It may contain many consonant sounds.

In composite words the syllable split occurs between the words that make up the larger word. Syllable division does not occur between digraphs and consonant blends.

| bathtub | bath tub | dishpan | dish pan |
|---------|----------|---------|----------|
| tinsmith | tin smith | dustpan | dust pan |

| | | |
|---|---|---|
| lipstick | upset | locknut |
| tinsmith | bulldog | baseball |
| lapdog | postman | locksmith |
| hatrack | softball | hotrod |
| caveman | landscape | milkman |
| bathrobe | tomcat | lifelong |
| checkmate | bagpipe | grandson |
| sunset | chopstick | springtime |
| hilltop | landlord | bullpen |
| hitchhike | gravestone | lineman |

The caveman is in the bullpen at the
baseball game.

## Syllable Division Between Doubled Consonants

The purpose of written doubled consonants is to indicate to the reader that the syllable division takes place there.

**Remember**: <u>a syllable can have only one vowel sound</u>.

| | | |
|---|---|---|
| rabbit | better | hello |
| fatter | latter | happen |
| bigger | comma | biggest |
| zipper | bitter | buzzer |
| holly | spotted | winner |
| supper | puzzle | puppy |
| trapper | attack | sadder |
| sizzle | apple | chatter |
| differ | sudden | assist |
| fussy | command | attend |
| common | nugget | fiddle |
| comment | ribbon | tunnel |
| riddle | dinner | shutter |
| nozzle | fibber | rudder |
| butter | slipper | wetter |

"My puppy is bigger and fatter and better than his little fussy rabbit."

## Syllable division between dissimilar consonants

Syllables divide between dissimilar consonants provided that they are not part of a digraph or a consonant cluster.

| napkin | nap kin | dentist | den tist |
| basket | bas ket | blister | blis ter |

| winter | goblin | compose |
| upset | formal | number |
| sandal | combine | under |
| sunset | campus | canvas |
| confess | orbit | wonder |
| doctor | picnic | welfare |
| order | corner | cactus |
| walrus | thunder | unfit |
| inform | border | content |
| witness | monster | former |

Whenever a single consonant separates two vowels, the consonant usually combines with the following syllable, leaving the vowel at the end of the syllable. A vowel at the end of a syllable is usually pronounced long.

| silent | si lent | label | la bel |
| motor | mo tor | soda | so da |

| | | |
|---|---|---|
| stupid | unite | began |
| virus | odor | focus |
| flavor | minor | minus |
| total | unit | rival |
| locate | lunar | cider |
| polar | donate | pilot |
| tomato | cedar | label |
| labor | potato | bonus |

Is that motor silent?

Please note that in many words the syllable division determines whether the vowel is short or long.

| Long vowel | Short vowel |
| --- | --- |
| hoping | hopping |
| diner | dinner |
| coma | comma |
| holy | holly |
| ruder | rudder |
| fiber | fibber |
| filing | filling |
| planed | planned |
| super | supper |
| taping | tapping |
| liking | licking |
| scraping | scrapping |

In the first column, the consonant goes with the second syllable, and the vowel is pronounced long. In the second column, the consonant sound goes with the first syllable, and the vowel is pronounced short. The meaning of the word changes accordingly.

# THE *ING* ENDING

In Level One, it was shown that a 'silent e' at the end of a word causes the preceding vowel to be pronounced long, provided that there is only one consonant between the silent e and the vowel. The same is true for the *ing* ending.

| | | | |
|---|---|---|---|
| hope | hoping | like | liking |
| file | filing | gaze | gazing |
| name | naming | dine | dining |
| rave | raving | wipe | wiping |
| rule | ruling | dive | diving |

If, however, the preceding vowel is to be kept short, then the final consonant is doubled before the *ing*.

| | | | |
|---|---|---|---|
| hop | hopping | sob | sobbing |
| spin | spinning | dip | dipping |
| mop | mopping | whip | whipping |

Whipping

| | | | |
|---|---|---|---|
| grabbing | buzzing | stunning | spinning |
| tugging | whipping | padding | dragging |
| shopping | canning | stabbing | fibbing |
| skipping | brimming | nagging | stirring |
| sitting | flipping | rubbing | setting |
| skimming | begging | slipping | dipping |
| betting | drumming | sagging | sledding |
| tipping | bedding | trimming | fitting |
| shipping | sobbing | budding | dripping |

His betting gave him
stunning winnings.

Some practice words with a long vowel sound in the first syllable:

| | | | |
|---|---|---|---|
| liking | filing | lining | rating |
| gazing | fading | hoping | dining |
| grating | raving | wiping | aping |
| naming | hating | dating | mating |

"I am hoping we will be
dining better at supper time."

Some practice words that have an *ing* ending after two consonants. Note that no doubling of the final consonant is needed to keep the final vowel short:

| | | | |
|---|---|---|---|
| walking | lifting | talking | jumping |
| planting | washing | brushing | singing |
| bumping | climbing | rocking | licking |
| dumping | pushing | swinging | sucking |

She did the lifting, brushing and washing. He did the talking and singing.

Some practice words in which the vowel is long.  No doubling of the consonant is used in the spelling, as that will not affect the vowel sound.

sleeping    bleeding

meeting    greeting

seeding    weeding

seeking    peeking

In the last two example categories above, please note that the syllable break is such that the *ing* forms its own syllable:

walking   walk ing      sleeping   sleep ing

The ringing clock was not waking the sleeping kitty.

## THE *ER* ENDING

The same rule concerning the ing ending applies to the *er* ending. To keep the preceding vowel short, it is necessary to double the final consonant before the *er* ending. Note that the syllable division occurs between the doubled consonants.

| | | |
|---|---|---|
| better | shopper | upper |
| letter | dipper | ladder |
| slipper | dinner | fatter |
| winner | bigger | drummer |
| summer | chatter | robber |
| patter | dresser | pepper |
| skipper | hammer | supper |
| stopper | rubber | glimmer |
| banner | bidder | madder |
| sadder | rudder | redder |

## SONG CONTEST

The winner gets
dinner, the rest
get no supper.

If there is more than one consonant before the *er* ending, then no doubling of the final consonant occurs.

| | | |
|---|---|---|
| helper | snicker | locker |
| farmer | jumper | rocker |
| flicker | tumbler | golfer |
| pester | sicker | sucker |
| ticker | picker | pucker |
| kicker | hacker | packer |

Please note that, when an *er* ending is added to a word in which the last two letters are consonants, the word is pronounced as a separate syllable.

farm er    help er        jump er    rock er

If the vowel of the first syllable is to be pronounced long, then no doubling of the final consonant is necessary before the *er* ending:

| | | |
|---|---|---|
| ruler | maker | baker |
| driver | fiber | diner |
| hiker | diver | super |
| clover | Dover | miner |

Here, the consonant goes with the *er* suffix:

ru ler        ma ker        ba ker

The above is an example of the general rule that whenever one consonant separates two vowels, that consonant usually goes with the second syllable, and a vowel at the end of a syllable is pronounced long.

sad                    sadder                    saddest

## THE *ED* ENDING

The *ed* ending has the same effect as the *ing* and the *er* endings. It causes the final vowel of the word to be lengthened if separated by a single consonant, the same effect as the 'silent e'. Note that the 'd' sound is simply added on.

| | | | |
|---|---|---|---|
| file | filed | wipe | wiped |
| rage | raged | pipe | piped |
| bake | baked | tape | taped |
| hire | hired | time | timed |
| size | sized | fire | fired |
| fake | faked | page | paged |

"I filed, typed, taped, and paged better, so I was hired."

In words in which the short vowel is to be preserved when adding *ed*, the consonant before the *ed* is doubled.  When the *ed* ending occurs after the letters *d* or *t*, the *ed* must form a separate syllable.  Some examples:

| | | |
|---|---|---|
| batted | matted | pitted |
| fitted | patted | potted |
| petted | budded | kidded |
| wetted | nodded | padded |
| betted | spotted | wedded |
| slammed | slipped | shipped |
| jammed | ripped | tipped |

Read the following list with the student and note that the *ed* ending is not pronounced as a separate syllable, but just added on.  The letter *e* is barely pronounced.  This occurs automatically.

| | | |
|---|---|---|
| robbed | stopped | nagged |
| bossed | hissed | fussed |
| skipped | bucked | miffed |
| buzzed | tipped | snapped |
| puffed | kicked | pinned |
| rolled | dropped | fussed |
| huffed | canned | kissed |

| | | |
|---|---|---|
| blessed | picked | planned |
| bagged | jerked | clogged |
| socked | blessed | rocked |
| jumped | crammed | locked |
| trapped | bumped | mocked |
| stuffed | ducked | slammed |
| packed | ticked | flipped |
| missed | shrugged | lacked |
| massed | whipped | tossed |
| repelled | mussed | smacked |

He had not ducked and was
socked and smacked.

## THE *LE* ENDING

The *le* ending causes the previous vowel to be long if there is only one consonant separating them. Here are some *le* words in which the vowel is long:

| | | |
|---|---|---|
| cradle | Bible | able |
| idle | ladle | staple |
| bugle | gable | maple |
| cable | bridle | Mable |
| table | stable | fable |

Mable left her bugle and Bible
by the table and got her bridle
from the stable.

The *le* ending also participates in the rule of doubling the final consonant to keep the last vowel short. Please read with the student:

| | | |
|---|---|---|
| hobble | riddle | bottle |
| apple | coddle | meddle |
| muddle | fizzle | little |
| bubble | puzzle | guzzle |
| cuddle | snuggle | cattle |
| bubble | settle | sizzle |
| brittle | fiddle | nipple |
| muzzle | saddle | prattle |
| paddle | dazzle | peddle |
| babble | cripple | raffle |
| rattle | battle | tattle |
| drizzle | kettle | dabble |
| nibble | dribble | scribble |

"This little bottle has so much bubble, dazzle, fizzle and sizzle that it will unsettle and puzzle the makers of brand X."

The *le* ending does not cause the final consonant before it to be doubled if that consonant is the second of two consonants. This is the same rule encountered already with the *ing*, *er*, *ed*, and now the *le* ending.

| | | |
|---|---|---|
| humble | mangle | jingle |
| ample | candle | fumble |
| pickle | tangle | angle |
| handle | single | jangle |
| simple | uncle | tackle |
| sample | dimple | temple |

| | | |
|---|---|---|
| stumble | pimple | mumble |
| rumble | humble | crackle |
| nimble | handle | jungle |
| fickle | grumble | bustle |
| dangle | hustle | sickle |
| freckle | rustle | pickle |

"He had ample space to handle the tackle and still hustle and not stumble nor fumble. It was a sample of his nimble skill."

# THE FINAL Y

The final *y* of a word has the same effect upon the last vowel of a word as do the endings *ing*, *er*, *ed*, and *le*.

Some examples of a long vowel sound when there is only one consonant separating the final *y*:

| | | | |
|---|---|---|---|
| hazy | baby | crazy | lazy |
| tiny | bony | nosy | ruby |

The consonant before the *y* must be double to keep the preceding vowel from becoming long.

Please read with the student:

| | | | |
|---|---|---|---|
| mud | muddy | sun | sunny |
| fun | funny | dad | daddy |
| fog | foggy | wit | witty |
| pup | puppy | Ted | Teddy |
| bag | baggy | sag | saggy |
| Peg | Peggy | mom | mommy |
| Tom | Tommy | pen | penny |

| nut | nutty | Tim | Timmy |
|-----|-------|-----|-------|
| cat | catty | sis | sissy |
| fat | fatty | rat | ratty |

| kitty | bunny | dizzy | penny |
|-------|-------|-------|-------|
| hilly | fussy | mommy | runny |
| caddy | paddy | fuzzy | giddy |
| muggy | lobby | Billy | silly |
| chilly | Sally | bully | taffy |
| jiffy | puffy | snappy | Jeffy |
| happy | poppy | messy | dizzy |
| stuffy | Danny | funny | muddy |

In the above list, the y is pronounced as a 'long e' sound. This applies when the words are pronounced separately, as when reading a list. However, when such words are used in continuous speech, the y takes on the qualities of a short *i* terminal sound, a sound that indicates nothing is to follow in the word, and that the word is finished.

Some practice sentences:

Daddy gave the fussy kitty to mommy.

The funny bunny had a runny nose.

It was sunny and muddy at the same time.

It was sunny when the funny bunny
hopped on the muddy path.

The letter *y* is the only letter that can behave as both a consonant and vowel. *Y* is a consonant only when it begins the word or syllable, and functions as a vowel elsewhere in the syllable. Some words in which *y* is a consonant:

| | | |
|---|---|---|
| yes | yet | yuck |
| yak | yank | yard |
| yell | yoke | yule |
| yarn | yap | yum-yum |

At the end of a short word, the *y* is pronounced as a 'long i':

| | | |
|---|---|---|
| sky | my | by |
| shy | fly | dry |
| cry | why | try |

This occurs because the word has no other vowel, and the 'long i' sound makes the word more easily intelligible.

Why was the shy
fly in the sky?

# SOME SYLLABIFICATION RULES

The concept behind syllabification is to split a word of more than one syllable into pronounceable parts.

Syllable breaks occur between double consonants:

| | | | |
|---|---|---|---|
| rabbit | rab bit | dinner | din ner |
| happen | hap pen | puppy | pup py |
| riddle | rid dle | summer | sum mer |

Splits into syllables generally occur between consonants, provided the consonants are not digraphs or consonant blends:

| | | | |
|---|---|---|---|
| napkin | nap kin | hamster | ham ster |
| kitchen | kit chen | lobster | lob ster |
| dangling | dang ling | butcher | but cher |

If there is only one consonant between vowels, the consonant usually goes with the following syllable, and the vowel that ends the first syllable is usually pronounced long:

| | | | |
|---|---|---|---|
| flavor | fla vor | locate | lo cate |
| cider | ci der | cedar | ce dar |
| donate | do nate | tulip | tu lip |

It would be nice indeed if this were all there was to division into syllables. There is a major exception to the rule just given. If there is only one consonant between two vowels, and the first vowel is to be pronounced short, then the consonant goes with the first syllable in determining the syllable break. The new reader will try it both ways. The pronunciation, either long or short vowel, that produces a recognizable word is correct.

Please read the following list with the student:

| linen | lin en | solid | sol id |
|-------|--------|-------|--------|
| modern | mod ern | rapid | rap id |
| river | riv er | tropic | trop ic |
| limit | lim it | panel | pan el |
| credit | cred it | visit | vis it |
| lemon | lem on | second | sec ond |
| model | mod el | modest | mod est |
| chapel | chap el | level | lev el |
| travel | trav el | shovel | shov el |

She did travel on a modest credit limit to visit the modern chapel.

# DIPHTHONGS

A diphthong is a vowel sound that results from a combination of two vowel sounds to form a new sound. There is a glide and blend of the two vowels.

### The *OI* or *OY* Diphthong

This sound is a unit, treated as one vowel sound. It is usually spelled *oi* inside a word, and *oy* at the end of a word, The sound is the same whether spelled *oi* or *oy*. Please remember that a syllable has only one vowel sound.

| | | | |
|---|---|---|---|
| oil | oiled | oiling | oiler |
| join | joined | joining | joiner |
| point | pointed | pointing | pointer |
| spoil | spoiled | spoiling | spoiler |
| broil | broiled | broiling | broiler |

| | | | |
|---|---|---|---|
| soil | toying | joy | toiled |
| toil | hoist | coin | boiling |
| boy | boiler | foil | point |
| coil | hoisted | coy | boiled |
| joint | moist | ploy | hoisting |
| boil | toiling | foist | enjoy |

The boy did enjoy putting oil
on the joint of the toy.

The *EY* is the least encountered of the diphthongs. It is usually spelled *ei* within a word and *ey* at the end of a word. Some words with the *ei* spelling:

| | | |
|---|---|---|
| rein | veil | vein |
| their | reindeer | reign |

The *ey* spelling of the diphthong is found at the end of a word. Please read with the student:

| | | |
|---|---|---|
| whey | they | obey |
| convey | prey | grey |

They did hold the grey reins to
get the reindeer to obey.

# THE LETTER C

This letter has no sound like its name. Before the 'soft' vowels *e*, *i*, and *y*, letter *c* has the sound of *s*. In all other situations, it has the *k* sound. Please read these *k* sounds of letter *c* with the student:

| | | |
|---|---|---|
| can | cat | cut |
| cot | cop | cap |
| cub | cup | cob |

There are just a few one-syllable words that use the letter *c* before *e*, *i*, or *y* to get the *s* sound:

| | | |
|---|---|---|
| cyst | cell | cent |
| cede | cinch | cess |
| city | cite | cyan |

Most one-syllable words use the letter *s* to get the initial *s* sound, and not the letter *c*. However, the initial *s* sound of letter *c* is common in multiple syllable words:

| | | | |
|---|---|---|---|
| cinder | cider | cipher | cigar |
| center | cement | censor | cynic |
| cellar | civil | citrus | cymbal |

If the *k* sound is desired before the vowels *e*, *i*, and *y*, then the letter *k* and not the letter *c* must be used:

| | | | |
|---|---|---|---|
| kiss | kill | kite | kid |
| kit | keg | keep | keen |
| kennel | kettle | kick | kept |

There are some words in which letter *c* has both the *k* and the *s* sounds:

| | | | |
|---|---|---|---|
| circus | cir cus | circle | cir cle |
| cycle | cy cle | cyclic | cy clic |
| cyclone | cy clone | cancel | can cel |

| | | | |
|---|---|---|---|
| accident | succeed | accept | access |
| occident | succinct | success | accent |

In many instances, the *cc* combination is such that each *c* has the same hard sound:

| | | |
|---|---|---|
| accuse | Mecca | occult |
| occlude | occupy | succor |
| accord | hiccup | stucco |
| yucca | tobacco | succumb |

Before an ending that begins with a vowel, the *ck* must be used. This is to preserve the '*k*' sound of letter *c*. (Otherwise, *c* would have an *s* sound.)

| | | | |
|---|---|---|---|
| picnic | picnicker | picnicked | picnicking |
| frolic | frolicker | frolicked | frolicking |
| panic | panicker | panicked | panicking |
| shellac | shellacker | shellacked | shellacking |

Some practice words with the *s* sound of *c*. Please note that in this case the *c* is always followed by *e*, *i*, or *y*.

| | | | |
|---|---|---|---|
| dance | race | spruce | chance |
| ace | space | since | mice |
| pencil | prince | ice | slice |
| fence | lacy | traced | pacing |
| trace | brace | mince | face |
| cancer | racing | place | icing |
| racer | pace | tracer | tracing |
| slicing | fancy | raced | rice |
| braced | bracing | dancing | price |

The prince drove his fancy racer on the ice.

# THE LETTER *G*

Letter *g* follows the same rule as does letter *c* in determining which sound is used, hard or soft. Before the vowels *e*, *i*, and *y*, the letter *g* takes the soft sound. Otherwise, the sound is hard. Practice with the soft sound:

| | | |
|---|---|---|
| ginger | gypsy | gentle |
| page | gym | stage |
| fringe | virgin | sponge |
| wage | ridge | bulgy |
| plunge | budge | bridge |
| gender | change | margin |

Some words with the hard sound of letter *g*:

| | | | |
|---|---|---|---|
| got | gal | gag | fog |
| gull | wig | hug | gaze |
| hag | gash | gulf | pig |
| gate | dog | mug | hog |
| gum | golf | gun | god |
| bag | go | fig | game |

Please note the effect of the silent *e* on the letter *g*:

| | | | |
|---|---|---|---|
| rag | rage | hug | huge |
| wag | wage | sag | sage |

Some mixed hard and soft *g* sounds:

| | | | |
|---|---|---|---|
| page | change | glass | gene |
| aggravate | gadget | game | gallop |
| hinge | gem | suggest | gamble |
| gasp | gather | ledge | gym |
| baggage | gender | glad | ginger |
| glide | gin | gobble | engine |
| glut | beggar | globe | god |
| gloss | gentle | gang | pledge |
| wage | dog | cage | glider |

As in the case of letter *c*, the *g* in each syllable is treated separately. The words gadget and baggage have both the hard and soft *g* sounds. The exceptions to the above rules will be explained later.

The gal and guy galloped while
the gentle dog got to tag along.

# The Race

Robert was the smallest boy in the class. This did not matter in class, but it mattered at recess time. Then the kids picked sides for games. Robert was the last kid to be picked for a side. Robert was fast and strong for his size, but the other kids were faster and stronger and much bigger. When kids pick sides for a game of basketball, the team with the biggest kids has the best chance of winning.

In time, Robert will likely be just as big as the other kids. His mother is tall. His dad is a big man. Even his older brother and sister got to be tall kids. For the present time, Robert is the runt of his class. But this is only in size. In games that do not use a ball, Robert can do just as well as the bigger kids. Still, Robert was the last kid picked for a side, no matter what the game.

It was almost summer, the time for the big bike race. Robert had not entered the race in the past, as he felt he had no chance of winning. But this time he had a plan for success. The race was ten miles long. It began on the close side of a big hill and ended on the other side. The only rule was that all the kids had to begin the race at the same place and time, and the kid that got to the finish line before the others was the winner. Robert made it a point to consider this rule with care. It did not state that the riders must keep on the path. His plan was to take short cuts. This was legal. If this did not occur to other kids, that was their loss.

The week before the race, Robert went with his bike along the path of the race. He noted the best places for taking short cuts. The path went back and forth a lot, just to avoid steep and rocky places and the river that went by the base of the hill. He noted that short cuts at these hard spots offered the best places to save the most time. The problem was that the short cuts went over sharp rocks and thorns that made cuts in his tires when he rode over them. When he got home, he had his dad help him put on extra thick bike tires. These made his bike less speedy, but it let him take those short cuts and not get flat tires from sharp rocks and thorns.

He went over the path another time to get his tricks prepared for the race. He hid ropes and boots in the bushes by the first steep ledge. His plan was to put on the hiking boots and scale that steep slope first, then use the ropes to pull his bike up after him. The path went a long way to avoid this steep incline, but twisted back like a snake to the upper level. The short cut saved a lot of time and distance. He placed ropes in three places like this. It did take a lot of effort to pull up his bike, which made his lips get dry. He decided to hide cans of soda with the ropes so as to have plenty to drink.

The big problem was getting across the river. That short cut saved the most time. He solved this by making a raft. It was ample to carry both him and the bike. This short cut alone saved three miles. He had his plan all in order. The race was at the end of the week.

There was a bit of a drizzle before the race began. It made the paths moist and slippery. When the race began, Robert let all the other kids get on the path before him. He did not want them to see him using his short cuts. It was normal for him to be last in line. But this time, this was in agreement with his plan.

It was fun to activate his plan. At the first steep spot, he got his boots and rope from the hiding place. He put on the boots and then attached the rope to the handles of the bike. He then went up the steep slope to the path above. He had to hurry, as the fast kids will be at this spot in a short time. He pulled up his bike, hid that rope in the bushes, and rode on to the next spot. He did not have to keep on the wide path to avoid tire cuts. He made little short cuts that went over sharp stones and thorns. His thick tires did not go flat.

He got to the second steep spot. He was not all that much in front of the pack and did not dare to rest yet. He pulled his bike up the slope to the upper path. He was able to see the kids on the path at the base of the hill. He was so far ahead that he sat on a rock and drank a soda and ate a candy bar. It was fun to be the pace setter. He was not able to resist a signal to the kids. He got on top of a big rock and waved to them. The forerunner was startled to see Robert, the little kid, in first place. Robert called to them to hurry and catch him, if they can. The kids put in more effort to go faster. Robert finished his snack and then went on to his last steep spot. The next time he called to the kids, he was on top of the hill. He dared them to catch him. They were tired but kept on with the chase. It was a hard uphill grind along the twisting path to the top where Robert was standing, smiling. The kids wondered at Robert's progress and pushed on to catch up with him.

From the top of the hill, the path inclined in a long, gentle drop that made it easy to go fast. Robert's next short cut was by the river at the base of the hill. He got his raft and crossed. The river was not deep, but it had a lot of sand on the bottom. No kid was able to ride his bike across and not get stuck. The raft was Robert's secret device.

The big kids had gotten to the top of the hill and went fast along the wide path that went to the bottom. They felt this was the place to put on the speed and catch up with Robert and pass him. After all, they had bigger bikes.

The kids kept up a fast pace. Robert was on the same path but on the other side of the river. He stopped to let them see him. The kids had to go over a mile to get to the bridge over the river. They wondered that Robert was so very far in front. Was he the best bike rider despite his small size?

Robert did not go so fast on the last stretch of path. He wanted to win, not make the other kids seem like jerks. He let them get close. The big kids did not have ample pep to catch him. They had taken the whole path while Robert had taken just a modest part of it. Robert felt it was better to ride smart than ride hard. His win was proof that a plan can make a task simple.

Robert won the race. The gang was more than a bit puzzled that he was the winner. They had not suspected that he was so strong despite his small size. The biggest kid in the class was in second place. The prize was a bucket of candy and a jug of cider. Robert shared the prize with the other kids. The kids declared Robert a hero. He did not admit that he used short cuts. If they had asked, he was prepared to tell his secret. They just assumed he was strong for his size.

Robert was not the last kid picked at recess any more. He was not big, but he was fast and strong. His size no longer mattered with the other kids. He used skill to help his side win. Robert was happy indeed.

## LEVEL THREE

## THE LONG SOUND OF LETTER *A*

There is a general rule that whenever two vowels are present in the same syllable, the first will be pronounced long and the second is silent. There can be only one vowel sound in a syllable. If one wants to sound two vowels, then two separate syllables must result.

In Level One, the long vowel sound was indicated by the addition of a "silent e" to the end of the word (syllable):

rat-rate          hat-hate.

In Level Three, the long vowel sound is indicated by the addition of a second vowel immediately following the first. <u>This second vowel is not pronounced.</u>

Letter *a* is often given the long vowel sound by the addition of the letter *i*:

ran rain   pan pain   man main   van vain

Some practice words with the *ai* combination:

| | | | |
|---|---|---|---|
| wait | saint | laid | maid |
| braid | bait | drain | tail |
| pain | train | mail | faint |
| saint | sail | gait | snail |
| hail | frail | brain | rail |
| jail | trail | Gail | paint |

| | | | |
|---|---|---|---|
| faith | gain | fail | plain |
| pail | Spain | bail | wail |
| main | stain | paid | grain |

The train waited for the cat's tail to pass over the rail.

At the end of words, this *ai* combination is spelled *ay*:

| | | | |
|---|---|---|---|
| lay | say | bray | pay |
| play | slay | stay | hay |
| gay | sway | ray | tray |
| spray | pray | may | day |

| | | | |
|---|---|---|---|
| clay | bay | flay | stray |
| gray | delay | repay | essay |
| relay | inlay | byway | allay |

It did pay to stay and play.

There is a reason for these two different ways of producing the long a sound. Originally, the sound of a in the word *hate* and the sound of a in the word *pain* were different. The *ai* of pain was pronounced like a diphthong. With the evolution of the language, the diphthongs tended to disappear and were replaced by the single long vowel sound.

# THE LONG SOUND OF LETTER *O*

The vowel *o* usually lengthens by the addition of letter *a*, giving the *oa* combination for the sound of long *o*. This second vowel, the *a*, is silent.

cot coat   rod road   Tod toad

Some practice *oa* words:

| | | | |
|---|---|---|---|
| soap | float | throat | boat |
| moat | oar | coat | loaf |
| toast | coach | load | road |
| oak | goal | toad | roast |
| coast | oath | loan | foal |
| coal | moan | croak | groan |
| soak | foam | roam | oats |
| coax | cocoa | boast | soar |
| roar | boar | whoa | bloat |

The toad rode on the coach on the road.

The "silent e" can be added next to the *o*, without a consonant in between, giving the *oe* combination to produce the *long o* sound:

| | | | |
|---|---|---|---|
| foe | toe | doe | woe |
| hoe | Joe | roe | oboe |

Joe put his toe on the hoe.

The letter *w* can sometimes take on the qualities of a vowel. Indeed, the w is a <u>double u</u>. It is therefore not surprising that the letter *w* can function as the second, silent vowel that makes the first vowel long. Thus, the *ow* combination can be pronounced as a *long o*, with the *w* silent:

| | | | |
|---|---|---|---|
| mow | sow | bowl | grown |
| fellow | blow | flow | tow |
| bow | grow | blown | mellow |
| shown | crow | low | row |
| slow | flown | bellow | throw |
| glow | show | snow | arrow |
| below | widow | elbow | mow |

The consonant letter *l* lengthens the *o* when combined with *d, t,* or *l,* to give the combinations of *ld, lt,* or *ll.* Please note:

| | | | |
|---|---|---|---|
| fold | mold | cold | hold |
| stroll | old | colt | sold |
| told | bolt | dolt | revolt |
| jolt | gold | volt | roll |
| molt | toll | scold | poll |
| bold | droll | troll | uphold |

In the above situation, the *o* is lengthened automatically in preparation for pronouncing the *l.* For fun, try to pronounce the above words with a *short o.* It is almost impossible, and the resulting word lacks enough vowel sustaining sound to be understandable.

This same principle of lengthening a vowel to make it more understandable is found in words like these:

host   post   most   ghost   both

He was most scared by both the ghost and the witch by the post.

# THE DOUBLE *O* (*OO*) SOUND

The addition of a second *o* does not give a *long o* sound, but forms an entirely new sound. This *oo* sound has two possible pronunciations, long and short.

Examples of the *long oo* sound:

| | | | |
|---|---|---|---|
| broom | roof | stoop | spool |
| mood | zoo | moon | droop |
| hoop | stool | booth | hoof |
| too | cool | troop | loop |
| drool | brood | root | shoot |
| soon | snoop | boot | spoon |
| spoof | room | tooth | fool |
| moose | tool | goose | loose |
| toot | smooth | pool | bloom |
| groom | gloom | proof | scoop |
| snoot | spook | swoon | stool |

Examples of the *short oo* sound:

| | | | |
|---|---|---|---|
| wood | good | hook | foot |
| hood | gook | cook | soot |
| look | took | brook | stood |
| wool | nook | rook | book |
| woof | shook | crook | wood |

In words like **blood** and **flood**, the *oo* sound is even shorter, like letter *u*.

**RULE: If the *long oo* sound does not make an understandable word, try the *short oo* sound.**

She took a good cookbook to the zoo to make food for the moose.

# THE *OU* COMBINATION

The letter *u*, when added to the letter *o* in order to give the combination *ou*, does not automatically create just a *long oo* or a *short oo* sound. There are in fact a total of six different possible ways of pronouncing the *ou* combination. These will all be explained in the next level. However, for the purpose of using the conditional mode in the Level Three stories, the *short oo* sound for the spelling *ou* will be introduced now. Please note:

could    would    should

These have the same sound of *oo* found in words like hood and stood. Please explain to the student that the *ou* in these words is pronounced as the short sound of *oo*.

Could I?

Would she?

Should we?

# THE *LONG E* SOUND

In Level One, it was explained that the addition of a "silent e" to an initial *e* made the first *e* sound long: **met-meet, ten-teen**. This same effect can be achieved by the addition of the letter *a*, giving the *ea* combination. The result is the same *long e* sound, even though a different spelling is used. Words that are spelled differently but sound alike are called <u>homonyms</u>. Some homonym pairs:

**meet meat    week weak    seem seam**

**deer dear    beet beat    peel peal**

**peek peak    flee flea    teem team**

**steel steal    feet feat    leek leak**

They could not
steal the steel
safe.

Some practice with *long e* sounds:

| | | | |
|---|---|---|---|
| keep | peach | sweet | speech |
| steam | seed | weed | sheep |
| beam | sheet | scream | seek |
| peep | bean | speak | free |
| sweep | screen | tree | bead |
| beak | yeast | seal | three |
| preach | heat | leaf | heap |
| wheel | weep | teach | stream |
| need | flea | clean | dream |
| keel | green | cream | tea |
| seen | feed | clear | reap |
| cheat | beast | bee | neat |
| lean | creep | deep | cheap |
| beach | see | leap | feel |
| wheat | east | greet | reach |

The *e* sound at the end of a short word is usually the *long e*:

## me  be  she  he  we

The preacher did speak of free speech under the green trees.
"Sweet dreams to all that seek to hear me," he screamed.

## THE *EI* AND *IE* COMBINATIONS

The *ei* and *ie* combinations are pronounced the same, as a *long e*. However, in our rigid spelling system, it matters how the combination appears in a word. Although the sound is exactly the same, one combination is right for certain words, and the other way is right for other words. The general rule states: i before e, except after c.

Examples of the *ie* combination for the *long e* sound:

| | | | |
|---|---|---|---|
| field | belief | ponies | thief |
| shield | yield | achieve | chief |
| genie | shriek | grief | relieve |

fiend     apiece     priest     brief

hygiene   siege      ladies     diesel

piece     Annie      niece      relief

After *c*, this *long e sound* combination is spelled *ei*:

ceiling   conceive   deceive    receipt

receive   perceive   deceit     conceit

The rule states, in its entirety: <u>i before e, except after c or when pronounced like a, as in neighbor and weigh.</u> The latter is the diphthong form of ei, introduced in the previous level. Some examples of the diphthong form:

vein      beige      sleigh     weigh

veil   ·  feign      neighbor   reign

The *silent gh* combination will be taken up in the next level. Of course, there are exceptions to the above spelling rule. Please note:

protein   weird      either     neither

foreign   seize      caffeine   forfeit

A second vowel in a syllable usually makes the first vowel long. In the case of *letter e*, the second vowel can be another *e*, an *a*, or an *i*. With letter *i*, the inverted spelling (ei) somehow got started and then frozen into the language.

Occasionally, the *i* of the *ie* combination is silent, as in the word **friend**. Rarely, vowel *o* used to lengthen the *e*, as in the word **people**.

"I wrote a piece full of conceit, grief, and mischief.
A thief deceives his niece,
his neighbor, and his
priest. Then, a wierd
chief seizes their fields
and reigns over them."

## THE LONG *I* SOUND

The *long i* sound in a syllable can be achieved by the addition of an *e:*

pie　　　die　　　tie　　　lie

Letter *y* at the end of a short word has the *long i* sound.

cry　why　shy　sky　fly

dry　sly　try　by　fry

In multiple-syllable words, the *i* achieves the long sound by its placement at the end of an accentuated syllable:

| | | | |
|---|---|---|---|
| bicycle | pilot | tidings | biceps |
| viper | final | microbe | dilate |
| migrate | silent | pica | libel |

There are two consonant groups that usually lengthen the *i* sound. These are the *nd* and *ld* combinations:

| | | | |
|---|---|---|---|
| blind | mind | kind | bind |
| find | hind | grind | mild |
| wild | unwind | child | behind |

The *i* usually has the long sound before the silent *gh*, which will be taken up in the next level. Some examples for now:

| | | | |
|---|---|---|---|
| night | flight | sight | fight |
| might | light | bright | blight |
| tight | right | fright | slight |

# THE *LONG U* SOUND

The *vowel u* can attain the long sound by the addition of *e*, thus producing the *ue* combination:

| | | | |
|---|---|---|---|
| argue | sue | cue | Tuesday |
| glue | blue | value | hue |
| due | continue | rescue | true |

The addition of *i* to *u*, giving the *ui* combination, gives the *long u* sound:

| | | | |
|---|---|---|---|
| fruit | nuisance | suit | bruise |
| juice | cruise | juicy | suitor |

Rarely, the *uu* combination is used to lengthen the *u*, as in the word **vacuum.**

The Blue Fruit Company

Motto:
Real men
drink juice

"On Tuesday the value of Blue Fruit stock did continue to go up."

# THE SCHWA

In everyday speech there is a tendency to reduce words to the essential sounds needed for understanding. Excess sounds become de-emphasized or are dropped altogether.

When vowel sounds are minimized in sound value to the point of being nearly, but not quite, dropped, the resulting sound is called a schwa. The schwa is a sound that does not sound exactly like any of the vowels but replaces the vowel in unaccentuated syllables. This de-emphasized sound is the same for all vowels: *a, e, i, o*, and *u*. The schwa is the sound in:

ago  item  sanity  cannon  focus

The dictionary symbol for the schwa is ( ə ). Some examples of the schwa:

## Schwa *a*:

| | | | |
|---|---|---|---|
| central | normal | total | beta |
| final | pedal | climate | signal |
| metal | drama | local | arena |
| algebra | cinema | cellar | gamma |
| dogma | delta | coma | cola |

(In some dictionaries, a greater loss of the vowel sound is represented by the symbol (ˊ). Example: butt'n. More examples will be given later.)

## Schwa *e*:

| | | | |
|---|---|---|---|
| tunnel | nickel | hunger | lender |
| bushel | blister | chatter | slender |
| thunder | glider | barrel | funnel |

## Schwa *o*:

| | | | |
|---|---|---|---|
| doctor | harbor | favor | color |
| terror | cannon | tractor | labor |
| motor | factor | Baron | felon |

## Schwa *i*:

| | | | |
|---|---|---|---|
| caliber | domino | decibel | minify |
| edible | unity | visible | engine |
| legible | levity | alibi | capital |

## Schwa *u*:

| | | | |
|---|---|---|---|
| fungus | minus | focus | chorus |

virus      campus      serum      fetus

How does one determine when a vowel is a schwa sound? One can tell only by trying it. If *done* is pronounced with a *long o*, it rhymes with bone. This is not a recognizable word. The next thing to try is the schwa, which sounds like "dun" and is a recognizable sound corresponding to a word the reader knows. It is surprising how soon this becomes an automatic response.

## LETTER *R* AND THE SCHWA

The weak vowels are *e, i,* and *u.* Before the consonant *r,* which is formed in the front part of the mouth, the 'weak' vowels *e, i,* and *u* are reduced to an approximate schwa sound, often represented in the dictionary by (~). Please read the list below with the student and note that the *er, ir,* and *ur* spellings are all sounded the same.

## THE *ER, IR,* AND *UR* COMBINATIONS

| | | | |
|---|---|---|---|
| perch | churn | girl | hurl |
| murmur | sir | herd | birch |
| lurch | firm | fern | church |
| fur | stir | twirl | skirt |
| whir | purr | thirst | her |
| curb | berth | jerk | hurt |

| | | | |
|---|---|---|---|
| burn | clerk | dirt | turn |
| first | shirk | surf | burr |
| churn | spur | bird | whirl |
| burst | furl | curl | shirt |

"The girl did twirl her curl."

"The surf did churn and whirl."

"It was her turn to burn the fern."

"The first clerk had dirt on her shirt."

## THE *OR* COMBINATION

In the *or* combination, the schwa effect on the vowel *o* is not complete, as the *o* is the strongest vowel when sounded. The *o* sound is somewhat modified by the *r*, but it is still distinctly sounded as an *o*.

| | | | |
|---|---|---|---|
| torch | stork | fort | sort |
| port | for | horn | thorn |
| porch | cord | form | lord |
| storm | corn | sworn | stork |
| born | pork | cork | sport |
| tort | short | north | snort |
| worn | fork | scorch | torn |

"I will:  mend the torn sport coat
get pork and corn for dinner
use the short tax form
fix the north porch
replace the worn cord."

## THE *AR* COMBINATION

Before letter *r*, the schwa effect on *a* is not complete, since *a*, like *o*, is a strong vowel. The *a* sound in *ar* is not like the *short* or *long a* sound but is still recognizable as a vowel sound of *a*.

| | | | |
|---|---|---|---|
| start | dark | lard | darn |
| car | bar | shark | hard |
| farm | yard | par | arm |
| marsh | star | park | bark |
| jar | tar | smart | spark |
| scar | darn | art | ark |
| chart | scarf | cart | lark |
| mar | far | sharp | stark |

There is a situation where the *ar* sound is modified by an initial *w*, giving the *war* combination that is pronounced <u>wor</u>. In this situation, the *w* causes the *a* in the *ar* to take on the sound of the *short o*. Please note:

| | | | |
|---|---|---|---|
| warm | warned | war | warn |
| warp | warranty | wart | ward |

"This march in C-sharp is not so darn hard to play. Start at the first bar and watch my arm."

# LONG VOWELS AND THE SCHWA

Please note that the *letter r* can have the schwa effect only on short vowels. It has little or no effect on long vowels. This rule holds no matter how the vowel is lengthened, whether by the addition of a succeeding vowel or by a "silent e" at the end of the syllable.

| | | | |
|---|---|---|---|
| fir fire | sir sire | bar bare | curb cure |
| par pair | her here | dirt dire | curl cure |
| far fair | car care | dark dare | purr pure |
| scar scare | star stare stair | | hard hair hare |
| hire | chore | wire | dear |
| air | gear | year | snore |
| more | wore | sore | fear |
| core | store | cheer | fare |
| pair | bore | boar | steer |
| chair | cure | near | peer |

As with all rules, there are exceptions. A noteable one is the word **were**. It rhymes with her instead of rhyming with here. Some other non-law abiding words are **some** and **done**, having a short *schwa-quality* vowel sound rather than a full *long o* vowel sound that should obey the "silent e" rule. It is the same situation with the word **have**. It should rhyme with rave and brave. It is frequently the very common words that violate the rules. However, because these words are very common and therefore frequently encountered, they are quickly learned and will present no problem for the student who reads frequently.

"Treat me, or I will scare the curl from her hair."

## UNSTRESSED ENDINGS

In speech, verbs tend to have stressed endings while nouns tend to have unstressed endings. In the case of verbs, the endings carry a lot of information regarding the person and tense and have to be clearly heard by the listener. This is especially evident in words that are both nouns and verbs. Please contrast the following sentences:

(1) He is a <u>reb′el</u>.

(2) If they don't get better food soon the prisoners will <u>re bel′</u>.

This section of Level Three is concerned with unstressed endings of nouns. These unstressed endings **usually contain schwa vowel sounds** and tend to sound alike. There is a tendency for lazy readers to pay attention to the beginning of a word and let the end of the word go by with only cursory attention. The student must be taught to **pay attention to all the letters** and not slough off the final part of a word just because so many endings sound the same. Only by noting all the letters can a student learn to spell properly.

# ENDINGS *ER, OR,* AND *AR*

Please note the schwa effect of these unstressed endings. They all sound very much alike.

| | | | |
|---|---|---|---|
| motor | color | trailer | glider |
| doctor | sailor | labor | slender |
| harbor | hunger | favor | eager |
| thunder | mirror | dealer | cellar |
| humor | chatter | blister | parlor |
| terror | error | tractor | similar |
| nectar | editor | major | calendar |
| regular | horror | altar | pilar |

## WORDS ENDING IN *ain, an, in, ine, ion, on*

These endings tend to sound alike:

| | | | |
|---|---|---|---|
| pardon | cabin | captain | region |
| curtain | raisin | human | champion |
| margin | genuine | ribbon | organ |
| religion | person | Britain | engine |
| robin | chaplain | carton | bargain |
| carbon | melon | chieftain | imagine |
| certain | satan | Texan | pagan |

The captain had been certain the engine was a genuine bargain.

# WORDS ENDING IN *le, el, al*

These endings tend to sound alike:

| | | | |
|---|---|---|---|
| pickle | grumble | final | puzzle |
| animal | nozzle | central | local |
| single | saddle | riddle | carnival |
| metal | musical | normal | nickel |
| personal | total | chuckle | signal |
| shovel | struggle | level | eternal |
| tunnel | bushel | tropical | needle |
| medical | weasel | cable | apple |

# WORDS ENDING IN *et, it, ot, ate, ute*

These endings tend to sound alike:

| | | | |
|---|---|---|---|
| pilot | minute | climate | socket |
| unit | credit | limit | carrot |
| deposit | spirit | orbit | nugget |

visit    parrot    scarlet    private

hermit    gadget    senate    pirate

The pirate kept her nuggets on deposit in
a private place.

## WORDS ENDING IN *able, ible*

These endings tend to sound alike:

sensible    irritable    edible    dependable

flexible    flammable    probable    incredible

eligible    favorable    deplorable    inflammable

portable    invisible    believable  predictable

terrible    available    impossible responsible

Irritable people make travel impossible.

## WORDS ENDING IN *ance, ence*

These endings tend to sound alike:

innocence    absence    appearance

attendance   residence   confidence

performance   ignorance   tolerance

abundance   annoyance   intelligence

sentence   providence   importance

deliverance  commence  cadence

The point is that similar, unstressed (schwa) endings tend to sound alike. It is important that the student examine every letter when encountering a new word, including the ending, even if he knows or guesses its meaning before completing a scan of the entire word.

# LEVEL THREE MISCELLANEOUS

## The Three Spellings of *To*

Words that sound alike but are spelled differently are called homonyms. The words *to*, *too*, and *two* are commonly confused because they sound alike. They sound alike for different phonic reasons:

**Too** has the long double *o* (*oo*) sound heard in words like **moon** and **soon**. It has the meaning of *in addition, also.* Example: *me, too.*

**Two** is a number. In Late Middle English (about 1500), the letter *w* tended to be silent when preceded by another consonant and followed by a posterior rounded vowel (e.g., sword). Modern pronunciation has restored the *w* sound in many but not all words containing letter *w*. This *wo* sound is indistinguishable from the *oo* sound as pronounced above.

**To** is a preposition. Prepositions represent relationships between entities, and **to** represents motion from the subject toward an object such as going <u>to</u> school. It can be used in the infinitive sense of doing something without limits, such as going out **to** play. Phonically, **to** should rhyme with **go** and **so**, but it is a de-emphasized sound, much like the word **do**.

The word **who** has the same *double o* sound of *to, too,* and *two*, in addition to the silent *w*.

The three homonyms of the sound **to** (*to, too,* and *two*) are so different that the context is sufficient to differentiate which meaning of the sound is indicated. The de-emphasized sound **to** is helpful in achieving more rapid speech, as **to** is a very common preposition.

"I, too, want to have two or
three dips of ice cream."

## The Letter *Q*

The letter *q* is never found alone in English. It is always found in the *qu* combination. The combination *qu* is pronounced like the combination *kw* or, rarely, like the letter *k* alone. Some practice with the *qu* combination:

| | | | |
|---|---|---|---|
| queen | queer | quality | quit |
| squeak | quote | quick | quilt |
| quarter | quiz | quantum | quite |

| | | | |
|---|---|---|---|
| quake | quart | quarrel | squash |
| banquet | quill | quack | quail |
| request | require | quantity | quash |

Please remember that the *w* is really a *double u*. Thus, it is not surprising that the *u* of *qu* takes on a *w* sound.

A daily quart of squash did it.

The KWICK LOSS PLAN let him shed weight quickly.

In some words the *qu* has the sound of *k* alone. This is because the *w* is often dropped in unemphasized syllables.

antique　　plaque　　mosquito

## The Letter *X*

The letter *x*, like the letter *c*, does not have a sound of its own. Most commonly, *x* has the sound of *ks* as in:

| | | | |
|---|---|---|---|
| mix | extend | explain | ax |
| extra | hex | fox | expert |
| exchange | oxen | excuse | six |
| fix | excite | pox | axle |
| express | box | expo | sex |

Letter *x* also has the sound of *gz* when it is followed by a vowel or by a silent *h*:

| | | | |
|---|---|---|---|
| exact | exhaust | exist | exit |
| exhale | exhort | exude | example |
| exult | exam | exhibit | exhume |

She: "It takes no expert to fix the exhaust fan and fuse box."

He: "No time. I did exchange six tickets for exactly sixty dollars. It will be an exciting game . We will take the expressway and exit at sixth street."

She: "I am exhausted."

He: "That is no excuse. Take an extra pep pill."

# THE FLUTE

Janet had a flute. It was long and shiny and had a very nice tone when played. She had gotten it from an old chest in the attic. It had been her dad's. He had played it in the school band as a teen-ager, and had not used it since then. He did not want to play it anymore, as he did not have time to practice and could produce only squeaky notes. When Janet expressed an interest in studying music, he gave it to her. He felt it was a good thing for a girl to learn to play a musical instrument.

Janet liked the flute so much that she kept it with her most of the time. She began taking lessons from a man who played with the city band. She practiced a lot and was quite happy with the progress she was making.

Janet's little sister Betty was not so happy. She did not like it that Janet had something that she did not have. She was resentful when dad praised Janet for the progress she was making on the flute. So Betty began to pester Janet whenever she played her flute. Betty rattled the dishes, banged her toys, slammed doors, and dropped things. She took her toy broom and used it to sweep the floor next to Janet. She squeezed her toy duck to make it quack. She did anything that disturbed. Sometimes she would even put a whole bar of soap into water and stir it to make a thick soapy foam so that she could use a wire loop to blow bubbles that drifted in front of Janet to prevent her from seeing the music. Betty's plan was to be a secret pest and annoy Janet so that she would quit studying the flute. Then Betty could get it and have it all to herself and get praise from dad.

Janet kept on with her music. She made such good progress that her dad gave her a reward. It was a bigger case for the flute. It had a red felt lining inside and a nice handle. Dad even had a big letter J put on the case. Betty got so desperate to get that flute for herself that she started to turn on the T.V. and the vacuum cleaner whenever Janet was practicing.

Betty finally decided to ask her dad for her own flute. If she could not beat Janet, she would join her. Betty did not really want to play

the flute as much as she wanted Janet to quit. Dad suspected this and got her a cheap metal flute that was in a wooden case. Betty took her flute from its case and played only when Janet was practicing, really to be the worst pest and annoy her. Janet felt that the only way to keep Betty from pestering her was to get far away from her. It was useless to try to get mom or dad to scold Betty. She would simply find other ways to do her tricks if told to stop some act.

Janet had to go to the garage to avoid a quarrel and to have a single minute's peace from Betty's noise and mischief. It was cool in the garage, but at least it was peaceful. Janet used her dad's tools to make herself a stool from the pile of wood that was in a neat stack in the corner. She took the best pieces of wood and put them together with some nails and then put her blue pillow on top to make a soft seat. Janet was pleased that she could get so much done in such a brief time.

Then something happened that changed Betty's attitude. The city band was all set to give a concert in the city park when Janet's teacher got sick. He was too ill to play in the concert, and called Janet to ask her to take his place. The music on the program contained some important solos for the flute, and the band could not play the music properly with no flute player. It was too late for them to get other music that did not contain parts for the flute in time for the performance.

Janet took her teacher's place, and played very well. The whole family was excited and went to the concert, and they were very impressed with the way Janet played. So were the other members of the band. They invited her to join the band. Her teacher had felt for a long time that the band could use another flute player. Betty was impressed that it was her sister that sat up on the stage and played.

Betty stopped her peskiness. She wanted to hear Janet play, and not have her go to the garage to practice. Soon, Janet was giving flute lessons to her sister. Dad took Betty's flute to the music store and exchanged it for a better flute. Betty practiced a lot, and hoped to soon be as good as her sister, and to someday sit next to her in the city band. After all, if two flute players are good for a band, adding a third should be even better.

# LEVEL FOUR

## DIPHTHONGS

There are only four diphthongs in the English language: *oi* (*oy*), *ei* (*ey*), *ou* (*ow*), and *ew*. Already introduced are the *oi* as in soil and toil and its alternate spelling *oy* as in boy and toy, and *ei* as in weigh, freight, eight, and neighbor and its alternate spelling *ey* as in they, prey, and whey. In Reading Level Four, the remaining two diphthongs, *ou* and *ew*, will be explained.

## *OU* and *OW* Diphthongs

The *ou* spelling is usually found in the middle of a word, while the *ow* spelling usually occurs at the end of the word. The pronunciation is the same with either spelling.

| | | | |
|---|---|---|---|
| house | mouth | count | down |
| cow | town | shout | out |
| bound | bout | how | foul |
| couch | spout | proud | noun |
| now | sour | growl | pound |
| south | found | our | howl |
| spout | scout | brown | pouch |
| owl | loud | frown | round |

| | | | |
|---|---|---|---|
| crown | clown | jowl | ouch |
| cloud | rout | stout | vow |
| grouch | sour | drown | towel |
| trout | bound | ground | pout |
| snout | prowl | sound | flour |
| crouch | gown | allow | scow |

Please note that the diphthong *ou* sound is different from the *ou* sound encountered in the words would, should, and could. In these words the *ou* is pronounced like the short *oo* sound, as in the words hood and stood.

"Down south in a proud town I found this sound,
Allow me to sing and shout and be loud,
My mouth will howl and my feet pound,
All hear me from the ground to that cloud."

# The *EW* Diphthong

The *ew* diphthong is pronounced by beginning with the short *e* sound and ending with the sound of long *u*. The *ew* sound is similar to the *ue* (long *u* sound of blue, true, cue, and hue.

| | | | |
|---|---|---|---|
| threw | blew | news | new |
| Jew | crew | slew | screw |
| drew | chew | dew | pew |
| stew | brew | strew | shrew |

Architects Limited

The crew blew it. They screwed up. When the boss gets the news, he will chew me out.

# THE *AU* AND *AW* COMBINATIONS

In the previous reading level, it was shown that the consonant letter *r* can have an effect upon a preceding vowel. The same phenomenon occurs when letter *w* follows the vowel *a*. A new sound occurs that is not a diphthong, but a composite, distinctive sound. This combination is usually spelled *au* in the middle of a word and *aw* at the end of a word.

| | | | |
|---|---|---|---|
| dawn | maul | jaw | straw |
| lawn | shawl | yawn | thaw |
| law | drawn | auto | taunt |
| flaw | haul | raw | fraud |
| flaunt | cause | Paul | claw |
| paw | crawl | launch | fault |
| bawl | draw | saw | pause |
| sprawl | haunt | hawk | squawk |

The consonant *l*, following the letter *a*, can represent a sound similar to the *aw* sound.

| | | | |
|---|---|---|---|
| fall | wall | hall | halt |
| balk | all | chalk | walk |
| ball | mall | bald | small |

| call | stall | salt | malt |
| tall | talk | squall | scald |
| stalk | qualm | cobalt | exalt |

"The facts are in my data bank. If Paul saw the auto stall, I will pause to draw upon the law to see if he is at fault."

# THE HIATUS

A hiatus is a noteable pause in sound that occurs between two successive vowel sounds in subsequent syllables. Because the different vowels utilize different mouth positions, there must be this lapse in sound while the mouth shifts from one position to the other. Please note the hiatus when the syllable break occurs between vowels:

**fluid** (flu id)    **diet** (di et)    **riot** (ri ot)

| | | | |
|---|---|---|---|
| trial | fuel | ruin | neon |
| video | pliers | giant | poet |
| trio | duet | radio | create |
| science | being | minuet | going |
| stereo | seeing | alias | friar |
| Brian | axial | pliant | triage |
| curio | patio | ratio | tapioca |

The hiatus causes confusion for many beginning readers. Problems occur when one must decide whether a two-vowel group is to be pronounced (1) as a long vowel with the second vowel silent, (2) as a diphthong, or (3) as a syllable break, with each vowel pronounced independently. Again, there is no rule. One has to try each way until a recognizable word results. This is not word guessing, but rather **a trial of limited possibilities.** For example, in the word *diet* in the above list, pronouncing the word with a long *i* and a silent *e* makes no sense. Only the successive pronunciations of the *i* and the *e* with a hiatus between them gives an understandable word. This is the case with all the words in the above list.

There is a situation in English where the language has been specially constructed to avoid the hiatus. It is in the use of the article *an*. Before a consonant, the article is *a*. Please note:

**a** boy   **a** truck   **a** car   **a** girl

Before a vowel, the *a* is changed to *an* so that the hiatus of two successive vowels is eliminated. This leads to better understanding.

**an** apple   **an** elephant   **an** ice-cream cone

**an** uncle   **an** old man

"We are going to create many trial stereo tapes for both radio and video. So, next the duet and then the trio will play the minuet."

## SILENT CONSONANTS

The beginning reader is often frustrated when encountering silent letters. A logical question to ask is why they are there in the first place if they have no sound value. The answer is that at one time these letters were indeed pronounced, but have had their sound dropped from the pronunciation of the word in accordance with the trend to simplify spoken speech. This is the same reason for the adoption of the schwa. The written word retains these letters so that derivational patterns can be discerned. Fortunately, there are consistencies that can help to identify silent letters in many situations.

### The Letter *B*

When letter *b* follows the letter *m* in the same syllable, the *b* is often silent:

| | | | |
|---|---|---|---|
| dumb | climb | limb | thumb |
| comb | bomb | crumb | plumber |
| numb | lamb | plumb | tomb |

When *b* is followed by a *t* in the same syllable, it is often silent:

**debt   doubt   subtle**

The dumb man's thumb
was numb.

# The Letter *D*

The letter *d* is often silent before the *ge* combination when the preceding vowel is short:

| | | | |
|---|---|---|---|
| dodge | hedge | ledge | ridge |
| edge | bridge | judge | budge |
| pledge | fudge | nudge | budget |
| sludge | sledge | smudge | drudge |
| badge | lodge | wedge | abridge |

Note, however, that there is no *d* before the *ge* if there is already a consonant between the vowel and the *ge*:

| | | | |
|---|---|---|---|
| revenge | change | hinge | orange |
| sponge | strange | fringe | binge |
| plunge | cringe | bilge | gorge |

The above generalization is useful in spelling. A *silent d* is inserted before the *ge* to ensure that the preceding vowel is pronounced short in the case where there is no other consonant before the *ge*.

Of course, the letter *d* may be silent in other situations, such as:

### handkerchief   adjective   adjust

Please note that **any letter may become silent if that word can still be understood by a listener without that letter being pronounced.**

The judge did not cringe at the strange case of revenge. He did pledge neither to dodge nor abridge the facts.

## The Letter *G*

When letter *g* is followed by an *n* in the same syllable, the *g* is usually silent:

| | | | |
|---|---|---|---|
| resign | gnat | gnarl | gnu |
| gnash | gnome | assign | sign |
| consign | gnaw | design | align |
| campaign | arraign | impugn | malign |
| feign | foreign | ensign | ensign |
| benign | deign | cologne | champagne |

The *n* in the above words is pronounced slightly differently from the usual *n* sound. The *g* is serving as a diacritic, an indicator of pronunciation. This is retained from the Latin.

Cologne
Avenue

"That sign is not aligned."

# The Letter *H*

Letter *h* is usually silent when it follows a *g* at the beginning of a word:

## ghost  ghetto  ghastly

Letter *h* may be unsounded if it is the initial letter in a word:

## hour  honor  honest  heir

Letter *h* of the *ch* combination may be unsounded if the *ch* is not a digraph:

| | | | |
|---|---|---|---|
| character | stomach | schedule | ache |
| chorus | chemical | chlorine | Christmas |
| school | anchor | technical | psycho |
| schism | monarch | orchid | pachyderm |
| dacha | Michael | mocha | mechanic |
| chord | echo | epoch | chrome |
| chronic | chaos | alchemy | Chrysler |
| cholesterol | chemotherapy | | chiropractic |

Michael the mechanic
scheduled time to put
chrome on his Chrysler.

## The *GH* Combination

The *gh* combination is frequently silent. Please note that letter *i* before the *gh* combination is pronounced long.

| | | | |
|---|---|---|---|
| high | sight | might | slight |
| fright | light | nigh | night |
| right | flight | blight | tight |

The sight of the ghost in the night might give him a slight fright.

When the *gh* is not silent, it is a digraph with the sound of *f*, which is explained later in this chapter.

## cough   enough   laugh   tough

The silent *gh* combination frequently follows the vowel combinations of *au* and *ou*. In the *ou* situation, there are six different ways of pronunciation that will be taken up later in this chapter. The following is, at present, for the teacher's information. After the *ou* combinations are taken up, the student may be referred back to this exercise.

| | | | |
|---|---|---|---|
| bought | though | although | dough |
| through | taught | sought | daughter |
| ought | brought | caught | fought |
| thorough | nought | borough | fraught |

## The Letter *K*

The letter *k* is silent when it begins a word and is followed by *n*:

| | | | |
|---|---|---|---|
| knack | know | knight | knuckle |
| knot | knock | knob | knowledge |
| knife | knell | knee | knapsack |

Sometimes the letter *k* is used to distinguish between homonyms (words that sound alike):

**night knight        not knot**

## The Letter *L*

The letter *l* is often silent when it is followed by another consonant in a syllable:

calf          folk          talk          yolk

salmon     half          stalk         napalm


## The Letter *N*

The letter *n* is silent when it follows *m* in a syllable:

condemn    autumn    solemn

column      damn       hymn


## The Letter *P*

The letter *p* is often silent when it begins a word and is followed by *s*:

psalm   pseudo   psyche

psychology   psychosis   pseudonym

Letter *p* is often silent after *m*:

pumpkin  empty      prompt    glimpse

attempt assumptive   exempt      preempt

Sometimes the *p* is simply unsounded:

**raspberry  cupboard  campbell**

Campbell's
raspberry
&
pumpkin
patch

Mister Campbell attempted to use the empty pumpkin as a mask.

## The Letter *S*

The letter *s* is, rarely, silent when it follows an *i*:

### isle   island

## The Letter *T*

The letter *t* is silent when it follows *s* and the *s* is not part of the *st* digraph:

| | | | |
|---|---|---|---|
| listen | whistle | fasten | chestnut |
| moisten | rustle | glisten | hasten |
| castle | wrestle | thistle | apostle |

An attempt to pronounce the two voiceless consonants, *s* and *t*, in succession is not possible without a hiatus in between. This is awkward in speech, and the *t* is simply unsounded.

The *t* is frequently silent before *ch*.

| | | | |
|---|---|---|---|
| pitch | hatch | match | itch |
| sketch | batch | watch | patch |
| ditch | latch | scratch | catch |
| stitch | bitch | clutch | fetch |

| | | | |
|---|---|---|---|
| Dutch | etch | botch | crotch |
| crutch | glitch | notch | retch |
| sketch | stretch | Scotch | snatch |
| stitch | witch | snitch | switch |

Some speakers prefer to pronounce the *t*, which is equally correct.

Please note in the above list that a *t* separates the *ch* from a <u>short</u> vowel. If another consonant separates the vowel and the *ch*, there is no *t* in the spelling:

| | | | |
|---|---|---|---|
| birch | punch | crunch | drench |
| pinch | parch | lurch | perch |

In the *tch* combination following a short vowel, the *t* has been inserted in the spelling pattern *tch* to ensure that the preceding vowel is pronounced short. If the *ch* is preceded by a long vowel, then no *t* is present before the *ch* combination:

| | | | |
|---|---|---|---|
| coach | broach | poach | roach |
| preach | beach | teach | reach |
| speech | screech | beech | leech |
| mooch | pooch | smooch | hooch |

## The Letter *W*

The *w* is silent when it follows letter *o* and is not a diphthong:

| | | | |
|---|---|---|---|
| snow | low | bow | hollow |
| show | row | stow | crow |
| mow | tow | follow | throw |
| flow | slow | below | widow |

The *w* can be silent following an *s*:

**answer    sword**

Letter *w* is often silent when it precedes an *r*:

| | | | |
|---|---|---|---|
| wrest | wreck | wriggle | wrist |
| wry | wrath | wreath | wring |
| wrestle | wrangle | wrap | write |
| wrench | wrong | wrinkle | written |
| writ | wrote | wrung | wreck |

The preceding examples are not a complete listing of all the situations in which a letter can be silent, although enough of the common examples of unpronounced letters have been given to illustrate the concept: **Letters are dropped when it is awkward to pronounce them, or they may be dropped in the interest of speech economy when there is no possibility of resulting misunderstanding.**

"I sit in the last row below the window. It was wrong to show the girls how to wrist-wrestle and wriggle my ears."

# SILENT VOWELS: SILENT *O* AND *U*

## Silent *U*

The vowel *u* is often silent following letter *g*. This combination is used to preserve the hard *g* sound.

| | | | |
|---|---|---|---|
| guide | beguile | morgue | guarantee |
| guilty | guess | guardian | fatigue |
| vague | guitar | plague | disguise |
| guy | guard | guests | guild |

There are some words that have a silent *u* before *i*:

**build   building   built   biscuit**

Please note that the *u* of *qu* is not always pronounced in the *kw* manner (quick, quality). Sometimes, in unstressed syllables, the *u* is silent and the *q* has the sound of *k*:

| | | | |
|---|---|---|---|
| botique | baroque | plaque | mosquito |
| antique | clique | casque | conquer |
| lacquer | racquet | torque | unique |

A guard at the building did not guarantee the guests protection from mosquitos.

## Silent *O*

Letter *o* is often silent in the *ou* combination:

| | | | |
|---|---|---|---|
| country | famous | young | cousin |
| courage | trouble | double | touch |
| couple | journal | yours | youth |

The *o* is frequently dropped in *ous* endings:

| | | | |
|---|---|---|---|
| enormous | hideous | gorgeous | famous |
| serious | generous | nervous | dangerous |
| fabulous | curious | desirous | marvelous |
| envious | aqueous | boisterous | credulous |
| joyous | aqueous | courteous | momentous |

"I'm curious if she's serious about that fabulous, georgeous, famous man."

"Don't be envious. He's courteous but not so desirous or generous as it seems."

# THE *OU* COMBINATION

This is the most difficult letter combination in English. It can stand for six different sounds. In order to appreciate the manner by which six sounds came to be constructed from only two letters, it is necessary to demonstrate the underlying logic and phonic principles for each of the sounds. The six different sounds of *ou* are as follows:

1. **The diphthong *ou*.** This has already been explained. It is presented here for the sake of completeness.

| | | | |
|---|---|---|---|
| house | south | mouth | plough |
| sprout | spouse | proud | aloud |
| shroud | count | louse | amount |

2. The short *oo* **sound.** This rule has already been discussed. Here, the second vowel of the *ou*, the *u*, serves to combine with the first vowel to give the *oo* sound. This is the sound of *oo* as in hood and stood.

could    would    should
tourist    detour

3. **The long sound of *oo*.** Since the *oo* sound has both a short and a long pronunciation, as already explained, the *ou* can also produce the long *oo* sound.

| | | | |
|---|---|---|---|
| you | through | souvenir | uncouth |
| caribou | youth | group | douche |
| soup | loupe | route | troupe |

4. **The long *o* sound of *ou*.** In this case, the *u* acts in the traditional way of lengthening the first vowel, the *o*, and remains silent itself.

shoulder    cantaloupe  carousel    dough

poultry     although    thorough    camouflage

though      boulder     comatous    furlough

5. **The short *o* sound.** Here, the *u* of ou is simply dropped, and the *ou* has the sound of a short *o*.

thought     sought      ought       fought

bought      brought     cough       mourn

source      pour        trough      course

6. **The short *u* sound.** In this combination, the *o* is silent without affecting the *u*. Thus, the *ou* combination is pronounced like a short *u*.

couple      trouble     young       rough

double      country     enough      tough

cousin      southern    famous      touch

adjourn     mucous      porous      pious

The above six ways of pronouncing the *ou* are important in discerning the approach to pronouncing a new word containing the *ou*. One has to proceed by **trial and error**. <u>This is not guessing</u>. With guessing, there is no choice between alternatives. In the *ou* situation, the student tries each of the phonic possibilities until he arrives at a sound that is a recognizable word.

The student should try this practice list of words with the *ou* sounds:

| | | | |
|---|---|---|---|
| house | could | coupon | borough |
| court | rough | astound | would |
| uncouth | fought | cousin | aloud |
| should | couple | boulder | thought |
| enough | plough | tourist | dough |
| brought | double | poultry | announce |

The famous band 'double trouble' plays enough country music for every couple.

## THE *EA* COMBINATION

There are three ways to pronounce the *ea* sound. As in the case of the *ou* combination, each may have to be tried before one arrives at the sound that forms a recognizable word. These three ways are as follows:

1. **The long sound of *e*.** The second vowel of a syllable causes the first to lengthen, and the second vowel is silent.

| | | | |
|---|---|---|---|
| meat | beat | wheat | cream |
| fear | seal | rear | each |
| neat | freak | beach | gear |
| meal | hear | beak | team |
| teach | dream | leak | spear |
| weak | heat | leap | reach |
| stream | real | peach | deal |

2. **The short sound of *e*.** Here, the *ea* combination is pronounced as if the *a* did not exist.

| | | | |
|---|---|---|---|
| heard | heaven | instead | dread |
| dead | ready | sweat | health |
| leather | thread | lead | tread |

| | | | |
|---|---|---|---|
| bread | wealth | feather | steady |
| head | meant | death | spread |
| weather | breath | meadow | heavy |

3. **The long *a* sound.** In this instance, the *ea* is like an inverted spelling, and gives the phonic sound of long *a* as if the combination were spelled *ae*.

| | | | |
|---|---|---|---|
| pear | tear | break | great |
| steak | bear | wear | swear |

As in the *ou* combination, the reader has to try each of the three *ea* possibilities and that sound which produces a recognizable word is the correct pronunciation.

**Special circumstances involving the *ea* sound:**
Before letter *r*, the *ea* sound is affected according to whether or not it has a long or a short sound. The long sound is unaffected, but the short *ea* sound is reduced to the schwa sound by the following letter *r*.
The *ea* schwa sound:

**learn   search   pearl   heard   earth   earn**

The *ea* non-schwa (long) sound:

**gear   fear   hear   dear**

**tear   bear   swear   pear**

"Instead of heaven, I fear and dread,
my dream of great wealth is dead.
I meant to search the earth but fear,
my heart's real meaning is but near."

# DIGRAPHS (CONCLUDED)

Digraphs are two-consonant combinations in which the resulting sound is unlike that of the letters from which it is formed. In Level One, the digraphs *ch, sh, th, wh,* and *ng* were explained. Now the last two English digraphs, the *gh* and *ph,* will be discussed.

## The *PH* Digraph

This digraph is pronounced with an *f* sound. Many words using the *ph* are of Greek origin, and *ph* is a Greek spelling for the equivalent *f* sound in English.

| | | | |
|---|---|---|---|
| paragraph | asphalt | catastrophe | alphabet |
| geography | orphan | hemisphere | elephant |
| telephone | gopher | photograph | symphony |
| physician | trophy | philosophy | pheasant |
| dolphin | hyphen | emphasis | pamphlet |
| autograph | nephew | emphatic | sophomore |
| physical | phrase | phantom | prophecy |

These are unusually difficult words. Phonic rules are necessary especially when encountering new and unusual words. If the reader does not have these words in his vocabulary, he will not automatically learn them from encountering them in his reading material. The student should be getting to the point where he can look up a new word in the dictionary and learn the meaning and pronunciation.

The philosopher heard a symphony on
his nephew's phonograph while he
began a paragraph emphasizing a
catastrophic philosophy.

## The *GH* Digraph

When the *gh* combination is not silent, it is a digraph with the sound of *f*. This pronunciation survives from a dialect of English and is found in relatively few words.

**tough   rough   cough   enough   laugh**

"Enough of this will cure your rough, tough cough."

## HOW MANY SYLLABLES?

It is common, in everyday speech, to drop vowels. This is done whenever there is a desire to communicate more quickly and there is little possibility of being misunderstood. In the following list, please note that if the vowel in italics is dropped, the word is then pronounced with just two syllables instead of three. Many of the vowels are either non-sounds when dropped or schwa sounds when retained. The choice of degree of sounding resides with the speaker.

lux*u*ry        asp*i*rin        iv*o*ry        marv*e*lous

desp*e*rate   nurs*e*ry      bound*a*ry   fun*e*ral

dec*i*mal      corp*o*ral     scen*e*ry     prosp*e*rous

More practice words. The underlined vowel may be sounded or go un-sounded at the speaker's option. The number of syllables in the word changes accordingly.

gen_e_ral       groc_e_ry       brav_e_ry       op_e_ra

num_e_ral       jew_e_lry       min_e_ral       soph_o_more

cam_e_ra        av_e_rage       di_a_mond       int_e_rest

choc_o_late     vi_o_let        hist_o_ry       batt_e_ry

gen_e_rous      lab_o_ratory    mem_o_ry        nat_u_ral

cent_u_ry       fav_o_rite      myst_e_ry       fact_o_ry

While some vowel sounds may be dropped from speech, <u>they may never be dropped from written English</u>. Ignorance of this fact is another reason for poor spelling.

**It is necessary to have a vowel for every syllable** by definition or there cannot be a syllable. Some syllables are quite long and have only one pronounced vowel. This may lead to confusion and an attempt to create additional syllables where they do not exist. Some one-syllable words:

| | | | |
|---|---|---|---|
| drowned | crowned | blessed | tipped |
| jerked | stuffed | crammed | flipped |
| trapped | maimed | clogged | slammed |
| planned | shrugged | jammed | grinned |
| bluffed | rubbed | snuffed | scuffed |
| clubbed | stubbed | bragged | stabbed |
| plugged | dragged | drugged | slugged |
| scanned | stunned | mugged | thinned |

This special *ed* ending, where the *ed* ending is tacked on and not pronounced as a separate syllable, was explained in Level Two.

Some two-syllable words that resemble three-syllable words:

monstrous (mon strous)
hindrance (hin drance)
attacked (at tacked)

burglar

reluctance

athlete

hungry

wondrous performance

lightning (light ning)
necklace (neck lace)
wondrous (won drous)
burglar (bur glar)
laundry (laun dry)
hungry (hun gry)
athlete (ath lete)

In the above list, proper division into syllables makes it evident that these are two-syllable and not three-syllable words.

Some three syllable words:

mischievous (mis chie vous)
performance (per form ance)
disastrous (dis as trous)
providence (prov i dence)
barbarous (bar ba rous)
maintenance (main te nance)
permanence (per ma nence)
reluctance (re luc tance)
religion (re li gion)

The point of the above is that **proper syllable division is necessary for proper pronunciation.** In encountering new long words, use of a dictionary is advised. Indeed, from now on, dictionary usage can be of help in both syllable division and pronunciation in addition to providing meanings.

## COMPOUND WORDS

One of the most consistent rules in both spelling and phonics concerns the formation of compound words. **The rule is to use all the letters in the smaller words in making up the compound word.** The syllable break occurs between the smaller words, and they are pronounced as individual words that have been joined. That is, they have a shorter pause in sound between the syllables as a joined (compound) word than they would if they were separate words pronounced in succession. There is generally a short pause between syllables, a longer pause between words, and a still longer pause between sentences. Of course, the longest pause comes between paragraphs.

Some common compound words. Note that all the letters of the smaller words are retained:

| | | |
|---|---|---|
| blueprint | applesauce | extraordinary |
| giveaway | safeguard | thereafter |
| sidewalk | blueberry | nevertheless |
| typewriter | baseball | wastebasket |
| football | sidetrack | whereabouts |
| farewell | pineapple | wholesale |
| moreover | homework | whereupon |

This rule of keeping all the letters of the smaller words in compound words applies even when it results in a doubled consonant where the words join:

overreach          granddaughter

beachhead          teammate

| | | |
|---|---|---|
| knickknack | jackknife | overripe |
| hitchhike | bookkeeper | cattail |
| glowworm | bathhouse | overrate |
| withhold | earring | overrule |
| nighttime | fishhook | overrun |
| roommate | withheld | powwow |
| misspell | newsstand | override |
| shirttail | hollowware | overran |
| overripe | coattail | interracial |
| overreact | posttreatment | roughhouse |

The above words may look somewhat peculiar, especially the double *h* in fishhook, but they are correct English spellings.

## MISCELLANEOUS

The word *one* is unphonic. It is pronounced as if spelled *wun*. It was once phonic, and has now kept the prior sound value while undergoing spelling changes. One is derived from the Indo-European word *oi-nos* (like the Latin-derived word unit). The *oi* is a diphthong containing the *w* sound. The word *i-nos* was shortened in Middle English to *oon*, and finally to the modern *one*.

Another incomplete spelling change is the substitution of *y* for *i*. Letter *y* was introduced into Latin at the time of the Republic to facilitate the spelling of words of Greek origin. The *y* spelling of words like mayor, crayon, and canyon gives the syllable a feeling of stopping, of a *yuh* sound. The *i* spelling in words like union and spaniel lacks this needed *yuh* sound. How much more convenient it would be for the beginning reader if the following words were spelled with a *y* instead of an *i*:

| | | | |
|---|---|---|---|
| Daniel | behavior | union | billion |
| junior | rebellion | onion | bullion |
| senior | opinion | spaniel | companion |
| battalion | medallion | pavillion | stallion |
| dominion | minion | vermillion | communion |
| behavior | million | materiel | savior |

The *ion* sounded as *yon* goes back to the Latin, where an *i* before another vowel was pronounced as the consonant sound of *y*.

Daniel's opinion is that the stallion is full of rebellion.

# The Restaurant

Andrew and his friend Pamela had working mothers. This means that they had no one to stay at home with them, because neither mom nor dad got home from his or her job until after five o'clock. The kids were neighbors. They often played together the entire day. Each mother would make a lunch for her youngster before she left for work. She expected her child to keep out of trouble and stay near the house until she got home to prepare dinner.

The two kids got into the routine of eating every lunch together. They would take their lunches onto Pam's porch and set up a table and pretend it was an outdoor restaurant. They had seen photographs of open air restaurants in such far away countries as France and Italy. The kids really didn't like the cold lunches left by their mothers and started cooking for each other. Andrew would pretend his front porch was a famous restaurant and take Pam's order. He would go into the kitchen and cook whatever she wanted and serve it, making enough for the two of them. Then, the next day she would pretend that her front porch was a restaurant. She was the cook and waitress and served him. It was great fun.

Soon some other kids saw what they were doing and joined in on the fun. At first they just let the other kids eat for free. But then they got the idea of starting a kids' restaurant. There were plenty of children who had working parents and were left home to fend for themselves for the entire day. They didn't like warm sandwiches and cold sodas any more than Pam and Andrew did.

It started out small and grew to the point that Andrew and Pam were serving as many as fifteen kids for lunch. Andrew was the cook most of the time and Pamela was the waitress. They didn't charge much. A bowl of onion soup cost ten cents. Bread cost five cents for two slices. A sandwich with slices of meat and cheese cost fifteen cents. For dessert there was a choice of ice cream, cake, or pudding or whatever else they could find in their mothers' kitchens.

It was nice for Pamela that her mother kept a well-stocked larder. On some days she was able to serve an infrequent treat like chestnut soup. Spaghetti with meat sauce was a favorite with their young clientele. On some days Pam emphasized a large salad that included celery, lettuce, tomatoes, sliced onions, cucumbers, carrots and whatever else she could find in her mom's kitchen. She put a thick mayonnaise dressing on the salad. For drinks, she had chocolate milk, soda, fruit juice, or hot tea.

The business partners did not tell their parents about the restaurant they opened. It was so much fun and mom might object and make them stop. But their parents began to notice that the food supplies were going down quicker than ever before. They also noticed that the dishwasher powder was almost all gone. And they noticed little chips and scratches appearing on their dishes quicker than had happened before. They were curious as to why but did not suspect the real reason.

It was on the second Friday after the restaurant's opening when Pam's mom had forgotten to bring some important papers to her office and had to go back home to get them. She decided to do it over her lunch hour. When she pulled her automobile into the driveway of her house she was astonished to see such a large number of children on her front lawn. She saw her daughter Pam in a waitress' dress, serving lunch. There was a sign stating that this was the Castle Restaurant, serving lunch only, just on weekdays.

She decided to stay in her car a moment and watch the children. It was a good group of youngsters, enjoying each other's company just as adults do in similar circumstances. They were getting into no trouble. In fact, she had never seen such a large group of children behave so well.

When Pam and Andrew saw Pam's mother, they got scared. But she was not at all like they imagined she might be if she found out what they were up to while she was away at work. They had imagined she would yell at them and all their friends and customers. But she was very polite and seemed interested in what they were serving and what it cost. She sat down and studied the menu and placed an order. She wanted cream cheese and olives on crackers and a bowl of chestnut soup. Pam gave her the best service. For dessert, mom had banana cream pie and a cup of hot tea. Her bill was fifty-five cents. She paid it and left a twenty-cent tip for Pam. She had to hurry back to the office and left the table as soon as she finished eating. Because it was Friday, she had a lot of work to finish at the office before the weekend.

When she got home that night, the lawn was immaculate. There was no trash anywhere. The dishes had been washed in the dishwasher and put away in the proper places. She noticed that her larder was less full than the last time she looked. She said nothing about the lunch to Pam, which puzzled her.

The next day, Saturday, Pam's parents invited Pam and Andrew to go out to lunch with them at a restaurant. On the way they stopped off at the supermarket to pick up a few things. Pam's mother took them inside with her and remarked about the price of food as she bought olives, cream cheese, banana cream pie, sliced meat, sliced cheese, and other things that had been on the menu of the Castle Restaurant. The kids were astonished at what those things cost. She also bought powdered soap for the dishwasher. This price was quite surprising to the kids. Mom also bought a few dishes so that the kids would see how much the saucers and plates and cups that got chipped cost to replace. Still, the parents didn't say anything about the kids' restaurant.

They had lunch at a regular restaurant. When the youngsters noted the prices, they realized how cheap their own prices were. The Castle Restaurant was the best bargain in town. There was no way anyone could begin to replenish supplies for the prices they were charging, or even pay someone to take the time and energy to prepare it. The kids were having fun but doing a lot of work and making their parents pay the bill.

After lunch, the kids told about their restaurant and why they started it. They were tired of the same food all the time, food that was left on the table for them to eat alone. They wanted to fraternize over lunch like adults often do. They did not want to charge the other kids anything but felt that since real restaurants presented a bill, they would have to follow suit. They now realized that they were feeding the neighborhood kids almost for free, seeing what things really cost. They were sorry about that. They had saved the money to buy supplies and now realized that it was not nearly enough.

Pam's parents and Andrew's parents talked things over, and then they went around the neighborhood and talked with the other parents who had kids home alone for the entire day. The parents decided to rganize a neighborhood club and hire someone to prepare meals for he children. They found a few grandmothers with nothing to do who olunteered to cook the lunches and keep an eye on things. Each arent would pay the real cost of the meals, plus a little extra for the vomen who prepared the meals. There was also a breakage fund to aave things replaced, if need be. The place for the restaurant changed very day, and each participating family got a timetable.

Things worked out very well for Andrew and Pamela. They had been getting tired of doing all that work every day, particularly all the nenu planning and then the cleanup. It certainly had been a vorthwhile experience in that they now had a better awareness of the effort it takes to go to a job every day. Pam and Andrew realized they were too young to have such a commitment and were glad to be out of the restaurant business. The best for them was that they were now a part of the gang that came to lunch and not just the cook and vaitress.

# LEVEL FIVE

## THE *TU* AND *DU* COMBINATIONS

### CONSONANT SOUND CHANGE BEFORE LETTER *U*

When the consonant *d* or *t* precedes the letter *u* in the same syllable, the resulting sound can be like the sound of the *ch* digraph in the word *choo-choo*

| | | | |
|---|---|---|---|
| future | mutual | nature | gesture |
| culture | creature | decidual | fixture |
| capture | residual | signature | feature |
| lecture | statue | adventure | nurture |
| picture | fracture | sculpture | torture |
| posture | punctual | furniture | mixture |
| pasture | rupture | fortunate | vulture |
| eventual | virtue | texture | textual |

It should be noted, however, that the *t* or *d* does not affect the *u* in this way at the beginning of a word.

| | | | |
|---|---|---|---|
| duck | dunce | duke | tube |
| tuck | tumble | dust | tuba |
| duce | dude | tummy | tune |

FRACTURED
FURNITURE
&
SCULPTURE
GRADUATE
INSTITUTE

"So I missed some lectures and took an easy schedule, but fortunately I did graduate eventually."

"Well then, what's the procedure now for an immature, unpunctual creature who pictures his future as a mixture of a furniture and sculpture repairman?"

# THE *TI, SI,* AND *CI* COMBINATIONS

When the letter *i* is preceded in a syllable by the consonants *t*, s, or *c*, forming the *ti, si,* and *ci* combinations, and this combination is followed by a vowel, the sound is like the digraph *sh* in the word she.

## The *ti* sound

| | | | |
|---|---|---|---|
| action | ambition | nation | composition |
| vacation | situation | initial | information |
| position | intention | martial | substantial |
| patience | operation | partial | construction |
| condition | correction | tuition | satisfaction |
| completion | collection | caution | conversation |
| reflection | occupation | portion | confidential |

## The *ci* sound

| | | | |
|---|---|---|---|
| gracious | special | delicious | especially |
| precious | suspicion | efficient | politician |
| official | sufficient | financial | commercial |

## The *si* sound

impression  recession  expression  intermission

admission  permission  compassion  progression

possession  confession  commission  succession

"I wish my financial condition were sufficient to ask permission for a substantial vacation."

## The *ch* sound

In the following words, the *ti* does not have the *sh* sound, but takes instead the *ch* sound. This is because of the *s* that precedes the *ti*. It is awkward to pronounce an *sh* (*ti*) sound after an *s*, so the *sh* is pronounced as if it were a *ch*. As explained before, this change in sound is in the interest of euphony and serves to avoid a sound gap between the syllables.

ingestion  digestion  congestion combustion

suggestion question  celestial  exhaustion

## The *zh* sound

There is a special situation concerning the *sion* ending when the *s* is preceded by a sounded vowel. It was noted in Level One that the letter *s* takes on a *z* sound whenever it follows an accentuated vowel or voiced consonant because *s* is the unvoiced counterpart of *z*. *S* is the sound that results from pronunciation without involvement of the vocal cords, while *z* is a voiced counterpart. Thus, in the list below, the *sh* phoneme changes to the *zh* phoneme.

decision    provision    erosion    confusion
revision    television    delusion    explosion
occasion    illusion    collision    conclusion

"Oh, the question, oh, the suggestion
leads to confusion and delusion.
A cowboy's life on television
is but indecision, exhaustion, and illusion.

## THE *SH* SOUND OF SUGAR

In some common words, letter *s* before *u* is pronounced like an *sh*. Please note the following examples:

sugar    issue    sure    insurance
pressure    assure    tissue    fissure

The above words are exceptions to the general rule, which is that an *s* before a *u* is simply pronounced *s*, as in the following words:

| | | | |
|---|---|---|---|
| subject | suspense | suck | suffer |
| Sunday | suppose | subway | suffix |
| sum | sunk | supper | super |

## THE *ZH* SOUND OF TREASURE

Please note the *zh* phoneme in the following words:

| | | | |
|---|---|---|---|
| measure | Asia | usual | treasure |
| leisure | casual | casualty | pleasure |

In these words, the *s* is acting to form the digraph sound of *sh*, but the vibrating vocal cords of the preceding accentuated vowel sound change the *s* to a *z*, thus changing the *sh* to a *zh* sound. This occurs naturally when speaking and is mentioned here to illustrate that **many pronunciations are the result of a tendency to economize in making sounds**

It's a pleasure to measure one's treasure at a casual, leisurely pace.

# THE PREFIX

A prefix is a syllable added to the beginning of a word to alter its meaning. One of the most consistent spelling rules is that when the prefix ends with the same letter as the stem of the word, both letters are retained. The syllable division is between the prefix and the basic word.

| | | | |
|---|---|---|---|
| dissent | reelection | unnail | nonnegotiable |
| reelect | dissatisfy | reedit | dissonance |
| reenact | misstep | unnoted | unnurtured |
| reenter | missent | misspent | cooperation |
| dissect | dissenter | reemerge | deemphasize |
| dissever | dissocial | misspell | misstatement |
| dissuade | dissemble | reeducate | dissymmetry |
| reenlist | unnoticed | cooperate | unneighborly |
| dissatisfy | misstate | disservice | unnavigated |
| reexamine | dissimilar | unnamed | unnecessary |
| dissonant | unneeded | reerect | unnameable |
| coordinate | misshape | dissolve | reestablish |

Some words without double letters, with the same prefixes:

| | | | |
|---|---|---|---|
| disappoint | recover | mistrust | unopposed |
| coexist | disappear | regain | disputation |
| disaster | rejoin | unkind | misunderstood |
| co-author | unfriendly | unlock | misinformation |
| co-editor | reconsider | unload | unimportant |

The dissimilar, misshapen objects tested coordination and prompted reevaluation to find unnecessary, unneeded, and unimportant reactions.

# THE SUFFIX

A suffix is a syllable added to the end of a word. This syllable can change the meaning of the word or give it a different grammatical function. For example, adding *ly* can change a noun into an adverb: principal + *ly* = principally. The same rule regarding double letters using prefixes applies to suffixes. Note in the list below that when the word ends with the same letter which begins the suffix, both letters are retained in the new word.

| | | |
|---|---|---|
| truthfully | cruelly | eventually |
| actually | successfully | naturally |
| finally | meanness | principally |
| usually | gradually | recoilless |
| skillfully | continually | incidentally |
| thinness | cynically | accidentally |
| keenness | brownness | suddenness |

Rule: When a word ends with a silent *e*, the *e* is retained when adding a suffix beginning with a consonant:

| | | |
|---|---|---|
| completely | likely | advertisement |
| absolutely | lately | commencement |
| scarcely | improvement | extremely |
| immensely | sincerely | requirement |
| severely | involvement | announcement |
| excitement | arrangement | encouragement |
| immediately | definitely | achievement |

However, there are sixteen common words that are exceptions to this rule of retaining the *e* before a suffix beginning with a consonant. Please note:

| | | | |
|---|---|---|---|
| probably | horribly | doubly | truly |
| possibly | wisdom | ninth | abridgment |
| incredibly | judgment | wholly | width |
| terribly | argument | awful | acknowledgment |

It can be instructive to examine the reasons why these words are exceptions. In the case of the words incredibly, horribly, terribly, probably, possibly, and doubly, please note the construction of the adverbial forms:

double    + ly = doublely     but is spelled **doubly**
possible   + ly = possiblely    but is spelled **possibly**
probable   + ly = probablely    but is spelled **probably**
terrible    + ly = terriblely     but is spelled **terribly**
horrible   + ly = horriblely     but is spelled **horribly**
incredible + ly = incrediblely    but is spelled **incredibly**

In the above, the final *e* and the preceding *l* are dropped because they are not needed for communicating the meaning of the word. It would be awkward to pronounce a word like *horriblely*, and it is simplified to the common (now correct) spelling, horribly.

**Please note the phonic explanations for these exceptions:**

In the case of *wide* + *th*, if it were spelled *wideth*, the *e* would make the *i* long. By dropping the *e*, one gets the phonically correct spelling width. The same applies to wise+dom. This gives wisedom, with a long *i*. However, the spelling with a dropped *e*, wisdom, is phonically correct, and is also "dictionary" correct.

In *true* + *ly*, giving *truely*, the *e* is unnecessary, as syllable division gives tru ly. Since the vowel ending an accentuated syllable is pronounced long, the correct spelling, truly, does not need the *e* to keep the *u* long.

In the case of *argue* + *ment*, giving *arguement* instead of the correct (dictionary) spelling argument, the *e* is not phonically necessary to keep the *u* long. Syllable division keeps the *u* long: argu ment. The *u* at the end of an accentuated syllable is pronounced long.

In the word *awe* + *ful*, giving *aweful*, the *e* is not needed for any phonic reason, and is simply dropped. *Aweful* and the correct spelling awful are pronounced exactly the same way.

Thus, of the sixteen words that do not follow the rule set forth at the beginning of this heading, eleven are seen to be phonic after all. Only the remaining five are truly unphonic:

*Nine* + *th* should be *nineth*, with the *i* long. However, the *e* is dropped with the *i* still pronounced long, making this an unphonic word, ninth.

*Whole* + *ly* should be *wholely*, with a long *o*. However, the *e* is dropped and the *o* still pronounced long, making this an unphonic word, *wholly*. But there is a shred of justification for the long *o* sound of *o*, since frequently the *o* is long before *l* as in words like old, bold, and told.

The three words judgment, abridgment, and acknowledgment should retain the *e* after the *g* to be phonically correct. This is because the *g* is pronounced soft, as if before the weak vowels (*e, i,* and *u*). The above words should be pronounced with a hard g from a phonic standpoint, but are not. This is another case of poor spelling getting to be so common that it becomes the "proper" spelling.

In words that end with a silent *e*, the addition of a suffix that begins with a vowel or a *y* usually causes the final *e* to be dropped:

value + able = valuable
snuggle + ed = snuggled
simple + y = simply
argue + ing = arguing

Some practice words:

| | | | |
|---|---|---|---|
| admirable | icy | shady | desirable |
| scribbled | lacy | wobbly | excusable |
| advisable | spicy | tackled | excitable |
| scary | trembled | continued | continuing |
| excited | admiring | trembling | encouraged |
| excused | arranged | arranging | encouraging |

The elephant was terribly wobbly and excitable and continued trembling in an incredibly discouraging manner. The argument is that someone had simply used inexcusably bad judgment in arranging the scary act.

The above rule holds for thousands of words.  However, there are nineteen common words that do not follow this rule but are nevertheless phonic because they follow other equally valid phonic rules.  The first five are:

changeable   manageable   marriageable
knowledgeable   chargeable

These words do not drop the silent *e* before the able ending because of the *g*.  A g before *e, i*, or *y* is pronounced with the soft sound.  In the above words, dropping the *e* puts the *g* before an *a*, and would change the *g* from a soft *g* to a hard *g*.  This is why the silent *e* is retained.

Please note the following five words:

replaceable   noticeable   traceable   pronounceable   serviceable

The silent *e* is retained before the *able* ending in order for the *c* to keep the *s* sound.  *C* before *e, i*, and *y* has the sound of *s*.  Before all other letters it has the sound of *k*.  If the silent *e* were dropped, the *c* sound would change to a *k* sound because it would be before a letter that was not *e, i*, or *y*

Please note the following three words:

courageous   outrageous   advantageous

If the silent *e* were dropped before the suffix *ous*, then the *g* would be before an *o*, and be required to take on the hard *g* sound.  For this reason, the *e* is retained when adding the suffix *ous*

Please note these two special words:
canoe  + ing = **canoeing**
shoe  + ing = **shoeing**
The silent *e* here is not really a silent *e* but functions to make the *o* into a

double *o*, thus giving the *oo* sound of soon and spoon. Thus, if the *e* were dropped, the *o* would have to take on the long sound and the word would not be understandable; *canoing* and *shoing* are not recognizable words.

In the word **hoe** + ing = **hoeing**, the root word is so short that to shorten it further would cause confusion. When one sees *hoing*, it is hard to tell what pronunciation is desired.

Consider the word **dye** + ing = **dyeing**. If it were spelled *dying*, it would mean something entirely different than putting a color into a cloth.

The same principle used in the word hoeing applies also to **acre** + age = **acreage**. The word is too short (*acrage*) to eliminate the *e* without causing it to become unrecognizable.

The last of the nineteen words that do not follow the rule in which the silent *e* is dropped before a suffix that begins with either *y* or a vowel is the word **mileage**. Again, if the *e* were dropped, the word is too short (*milage*) to be recognized for its basic meaning.

Is it courageous, outrageous, or advantageous for a marriageable, knowledgeable woman to be so changeable in planning?

When a suffix is added to a word ending with a *y*, there are two simple rules
(1) **Keep the final *y* when adding a suffix that begins with the letter *i*.**
(2) **Before all other suffixes, change the letter *y* to *i*.**
Please note:

vary + ing = varying     qualify + ed  = qualified
vary + ed  = varied      qualify + ing = qualifying

The reason for this is in the nature of the letter *y*. *Y* has the aspect of a terminal sound, while the *i* has the aspect of a propelling sound. The *y* is used to ensure a pause before the *i*, so that two syllables will be sounded and there will not be a blending of a double *i* as occurs in the word *skiing*.
Some practice words follow. Please pay attention to the spelling and see if the student can reconstruct the word minus the suffix. For example, luckily is *lucky + ly*.

| | | | |
|---|---|---|---|
| busily | furious | emptiness | hungrily |
| steadily | heavily | occupying | occupied |
| luckily | magnified | holiness | mysterious |
| studied | specified | studying | magnifying |
| loneliness | various | modifying | modified |
| glorious | liveliness | studious | friendliness |

A rather interesting rule occurs concerning the addition of the suffix *ly* to a word ending with *c*. **Instead of adding *ly*, the proper suffix is *ally*.** Please note, however, that the extra *al* of the *ally* suffix is not pronounced:

**automatic automatically   drastic drastically**

artistically     musically     critically
specifically     magically     frantically

| electrically | basically | typically |
| economically | comically | majestically |
| scientifically | politically | systematically |
| ironically | drastically | logically |

The only exception to the above rule is the word **publicly**.

Please note that in syllabification the suffix is usually treated as a separate syllable.

walk ing   state ment   love ly   advis able   final ly

Basically, critically, and scientifically,
it isn't so.  But artistically, comically,
and magically, it works.

# NOUN OR VERB?

One of the most basic principles of phonics is that a syllable is an independent part of a word. **The pronunciation of one syllable will not affect the pronunciation of adjacent syllables.** That which will have an effect on the word as a whole is the amount of stress given to each syllable. Stress emphasis on a syllable will change a voiceless consonant into a voiced counterpart, or change a schwa vowel sound into a full, long vowel sound.

Speech involves rhythm, and often this rhythm is critical in determining important accents upon syllables, essential to understanding. Nowhere is this better illustrated than in the use of the same word as a noun or as a verb. In this situation, it is the noun that has the accent on an early syllable, and the verb that has the accent on the last syllable. Please note:

## Record

*He bought a record at the store.* Here the accent is on the first syllable, re′cord. Record is a noun.
*Use the tape machine to record that.* Here, the accent is on the second syllable, re cord′. Record is a verb.

## Content

*The content of the book is secret.* Con′tent is a noun.
*The children are content at last.* Con tent′ is a verb.

## Object

*What is the object of your visit?* Ob′ject is a noun.
*I object to the tax increase.* Ob ject′ is a verb.

The judge did convict the defendant of the crime.
The defendant went to prison as a convict.

Convict

*He is a convict in the state jail.*  Con'vict is a noun.
*The jury did convict him of the crime.*  Con vict' is a verb.

## Rebel

*He is known to be a rebel.* Reb′el is a noun.
*The troops did not rebel.* Re bel′ is a verb.

## Excuse

*What is your excuse?* Excuse as a noun has a soft sound of *s*.
*Please excuse me.* Excuse as a verb has a voiced sound of *s*, sounded like the letter *z*, because the accent falls on the latter syllable and changes the *s* to a *z* sound.

## Detail

*Please note the detail in this painting.* Detail as a noun is de′tail. The *e* is pronounced long, as are vowels that end an accentuated syllable.
*Please detail your activities of last week.* De tail′ as a verb has a *short e* in the first (unaccented) syllable

As an optional exercise, the teacher may have the student write sentences in which the same word is used first as a noun and then as a verb, noting the accents and pronunciation changes between the same word used in these two different contexts. Here is a list:

| | | | |
|---|---|---|---|
| abstract | collect | accent | annex |
| advance | contrast | address | export |
| retail | convert | conflict | conduct |
| survey | consort | contract | contest |
| cement | import | combat | ferment |
| increase | subject | survey | extract |
| bargain | decrease | torment | permit |

# ACCENT AND THE DOUBLED CONSONANT

Not all words change stress emphasis when they are used as either nouns or verbs. In Level Two, it was shown that certain endings added to a word require that the consonant be doubled if the preceding vowel is to be kept short. The most common of these endings are *ed* and *ing*: commit, committed, committing. There is, however, one more condition to be considered regarding the doubling of the final consonant before the endings *ed* and *ing*. Please note:

## refer refe<u>rr</u>ing     color colo<u>r</u>ing

The word refer doubles the final consonant before a suffix beginning with a vowel. The word color changes to coloring without doubling the final consonant. Why?

The answer depends upon where the accent occurs in the word. There is a doubling of the final consonant of a word when adding a suffix that begins with a vowel only if:

(1)  The vowel ends with a single consonant preceded by a vowel,
(2)  The suffix begins with a vowel, and
(3)  The word is accentuated on the last syllable.

The only new information in the above list is the third condition, concerning the accentuated syllable. Please note the syllable accent:

| | | | |
|---|---|---|---|
| prefer | preferring | preferred | (pre fer´) |
| honor | honoring | honored | (hon´or) |
| propel | propelled | propelling | (pro pel´) |
| rumor | rumored | rumoring | (ru´mor) |

Some additional words for the student to consider:

| | | |
|---|---|---|
| occur | occurring | occurred |
| confer | conferring | conferred |
| commit | committed | committing |
| differ | differed | differing |
| cancel | canceled | canceling |
| shovel | shoveled | shoveling |
| | | |
| label | labeled | labeling |
| pilot | piloted | piloting |
| expel | expelled | expelling |
| acquit | acquitted | acquitting |
| patrol | patrolled | patrolling |
| control | controlled | controlling |

The teacher preferred expelling the boys who committed the offense. However, the principal conferred with the boys and acquitted them, canceling the expulsion.

# PLURALS

In order to understand the phonic principles behind the formation of plurals, it is necessary to start with a short discussion of equivalent voiced and unvoiced consonants. In English, there are five such pairs:

| **Voiced** | **Unvoiced** |
|---|---|
| v  (vast) | f  (fast) |
| g  (gin) | k  (kin) |
| b  (bit) | p  (pit) |
| d  (dome) | t  (tome) |
| z  (zinc) | s  (sink) |

These pairs of letters are equivalent in that **if one uses the mouth position for a voiced consonant, but pronounces it without using the vocal cords, the unvoiced counterpart will be sounded, and vice-versa.** This has previously been demonstrated in regard to the pairs *f - v, s - z,* and *t - d.* For example, note the words *of* and *off.*

In Reading Level One, it was noted that there are two pronunciations of the final *s.* After the unvoiced consonants *f, k, p,* and *t,* the *s* is pronounced voiceless:

cats      mats      ducks      racks
huffs      cuffs      hips      bumps

After voiced consonants, the *s* takes on its voiced equivalent, the *z* sound:

| | | | |
|---|---|---|---|
| runs | tubs | wigs | rugs |
| ribs | digs | dogs | bells |
| hums | hogs | jogs | wins |
| hugs | lugs | hills | bugs |

The reason for this lies in the nature of vocal cord vibration. Unvoiced consonants do not get the vocal cords vibrating in order to make their sound, and the vocal cords do not start up just to vibrate for one terminal sound. This is why there is the soft (unvoiced) sound after *f, k, p,* and *t*.

However, after a voiced consonant, the *s* cannot be pronounced in an unvoiced manner. In order for the speaker to pronounce the final *s* as an *s* (unvoiced), the preceding consonant must drop its voiced aspect. But if this is done, note what happens:

Pronounce bags with a soft s and it becomes *backs*. The same thing occurs with tags - it becomes *tacks*. Bugs becomes *bucks*.

Please look once more at the list of voiced and unvoiced consonants at the beginning of this section. The letter *k* is the unvoiced equivalent of *g*. This explains why one cannot pronounce any *ink* word without it sounding like *ingk*. Try pronouncing pink, stink, and think and they will always sound like "pingk", "stingk", and "thingk". This is because the vocalized consonant *n* converts the unvoiced consonant *k* into its voiced equivalent, letter *g*.

Cubs pronounced with an attempt to preserve the soft *s* becomes *cups*. Tubs becomes *tups*. Cobs becomes *cops*. The reason for this is that the equivalent unvoiced counterpart of *b* is *p*.

Try pronouncing beds with a soft *s*. It will sound like *bets*. Pods becomes *pots*. Dads becomes *dats*.

## A PRONUNCIATION LESSON

"Repeat after me: ink, pink, stink, think."

"Ingk, pingk, stingk, thingk."

The plural of a noun is formed by adding *s* whenever the *s* unites readily with the word without forming an extra syllable:

boy boys    book books    uniform uniforms

The addition of *s* to a noun is the most common way of forming the plural:

| | | | |
|---|---|---|---|
| picnics | answers | hinges | foes |
| times | promises | messages | forests |
| toys | doors | strangers | orchards |
| chances | chairs | lights | beds |

In words in which the *s* cannot readily unite, an *es* must be used to form the plural. This occurs after the words that end in *s*, *x* (*ks*), and the digraphs *sh* and *ch*. These are unvoiced sounds, and the *s* cannot be added on. Because an *es* is needed, an extra syllable results.

alias-aliases  actress-actresses  scratch-scratches

| | | | |
|---|---|---|---|
| speeches | brushes | wishes | arches |
| boxes | branches | prefixes | suffixes |
| bushes | foxes | surpluses | compasses |
| reflexes | matches | gases | sandwiches |
| eyelashes | churches | marshes | mixes |

Please note that when the *ch* is not a digraph, but is the sound of *k* with a silent *h*, then the plural takes just an *s*.

stomachs  monarchs  epochs

The most unusual plural is that which is sometimes formed after *f* and *fe*. In most cases, the plural simply adds an *s*:

cliff cliffs  dwarf dwarfs  giraffe giraffes

| | | | |
|---|---|---|---|
| bailiffs | bluffs | briefs | chefs |
| gulfs | sheriffs | chiefs | griefs |
| clefs | cuffs | plaintiffs | reliefs |
| proofs | puffs | reefs | mischiefs |
| beliefs | whiffs | waifs | safes |

However, in certain words in which the *f* or *fe* is preceded by a long vowel or an *l*, and the word is derived from a direct English source, the *f* and *fe* change to *ves* in forming the plural.

calf calves    half halves    elf elves

life lives    wife wives    shelf shelves

wolf wolves    self selves    thief thieves

leaf leaves    loaf loaves    knife knives

A thief                    Two thieves

The words in the above list are examples of the unvoiced *f* becoming the voiced *v*. When this happens, the accent stress shifts to the end of the word. In a few words, however, the plural may be formed in either way:

wharf wharfs wharves    scarf scarfs scarves

Nouns ending with *y* take their plurals in one of two ways.
(1) When the word ends with *y* preceded by a vowel, add *s*:

alley alleys     attorney attorneys

boy boys     pulley pulleys

| chimneys | donkeys | journeys | keys |
| kidneys | whiskeys | monkeys | trolleys |
| turkeys | valleys | convoys | abbeys |

(2) When the final *y* of the word is preceded by a consonant, the *y* is changed to an *i* and *es* is added to form the plural:

ally allies     berry berries

body bodies     tragedy tragedies

| comedies | cities | skies | follies |
| countries | lilies | daisies | stories |
| quantities | juries | pastries | enemies |
| territories | ladies | luxuries | policies |

This change in spelling for the plural is to avoid the pause aspect of the pronunciation of letter *y*. Letter *i* propels the sound so that the plural form *ies* makes only one syllable.

# THE TWO SOUNDS OF LETTER *X*

It was previously noted that the letter *x* does not have a sound of its own, but is pronounced with either the sound of *ks* or *gz*.

## The *ks* sound of letter *x*

mix  hex  fix  axle  oxen  extra  fox

## The *gz* sound of letter *x*

exact  exhaust  exist  example  exam  exude

Please note that *ks* is the unvoiced equivalent of *gz*. If there is a succeeding stressed vowel or a silent *h*, the unvoiced *ks* sound becomes the voiced *gz*.

He should fix that exhaust. It exudes extra pollution.

# Expanding Your Child's Horizons

by Dr. Art Atwell

### *A Whole Learning Activities Book for Parents & Teachers!*

In many ways, we as parents and teachers can enable our children to scale mountain peaks and to taste stardust—like great eagles they can learn to soar in the sky above the mountain tops. We are their most important influence. We can help them make it happen. They can reach up and touch rainbows if they (and we) believe they can!

ISBN  0-933025-28-9          $12.95

# ANOTHER EDUCATIONAL BOOK
# BY BLUE BIRD PUBLISHING

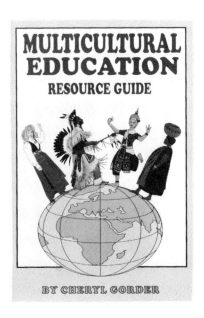

## *Multicultural Education Resource Guide*
## by Cheryl Gorder

Resources for parents & teachers for use in multicultural education: curriculums, textbooks, toys, games, software, audio-visual materials, music education, teacher and student services, cultural events, magazines, and newsletters.

ISBN  0-933025-37-8          $12.95

# Divorced Dad's Handbook
by Robert Bernstein and Richard Worth

*As seen in New York Times
and Publishers Weekly!!*

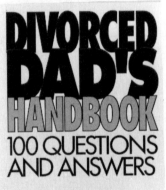

**New York Times**—"The handbook is aimed at helping men to hang in there."
**Salem Day**—"A field guide for divorced men who want to remain part of their children's lives."
**Menstuff**—"The book is aimed at men who want to maintain a fulfilling relationship with their children following a divorce but may not know exactly how to do it successfully."

**Easy to follow question-answer format.**

ISBN  0-933025-40-8              $12.95

## ANOTHER PARENTING BOOK
## BY BLUE BIRD PUBLISHING

*Heartful Parenting:*
*Connected Parenting & Emotional Intelligence*
by  David E. Myers, Ph.D.

There is a secret ingredient to successful parenting. That ingredient is connectedness. The bestseller *Emotional Intelligence* by Daniel Goleman shows how emotional intelligence affects people's lives. Dr. Myers goes further in this insightful book that shows, in a very practical manner, how to truly become connected with your children.

ISBN  0-933025-51-3                    $14.95

# Home Schools: An Alternative
### 4th edition

A homeschooling bestseller!
ISBN 0-933025-47-5    $12.95

How has homeschooling evolved from a radical idea into a mainstream movement? Cheryl Gorder explains how. Why is homeschooling better for children psychologically than public schools? Cheryl Gorder explains why. How should a parent get started, if they are interested in homeschooling? Cheryl Gorder shows how.

This homeschooling classic is now in its fourth edition. It has been reviewed over the years by *Library Journal, Booklist, Small Press Book Review, Book Reader, The Family Learing Connection, Home Education Magazine, The Big Book of Home Learning, Parent & Teachers of Gifted Children, Marriage & Family Living*, and many more.

# ANOTHER HOME SCHOOL BOOK
# BY BLUE BIRD PUBLISHING

## *HOME EDUCATION RESOURCE GUIDE*
### by  Cheryl Gorder   (4th Edition)

Hundreds of important addresses for home schooling materials and resources. Updated 1996. Includes resources for: legal information about home education; correspondence courses; textbooks; educational toys, games, & software; Bible education materials; child-training books; how-to-home-school books; help for the handicapped students and parents; home business ideas; home school support groups; speakers & seminars; audio-visual materials, and more!

ISBN  0-933025-48-3                    $12.95

# ORDER FORM

To order more books from Blue Bird Publishing, use this handy order form. For free catalog, write to address below or check Web site: http://www.bluebird1.co

| | |
|---|---|
| _____ *Homeless! Without Addresses in America* | $11.95 |
| _____ *Home Schools: An Alternative* (4th edition) | $12.95 |
| _____ *Home Education Resource Guide* (4th ed.) | $12.95 |
| _____ *Heartful Parenting* | $14.95 |
| _____ *Home Business Resource Guide* | $11.95 |
| _____ *Dr. Christman's Learn-to-Read Book* | $15.95 |
| _____ *Look Inside: Affirmations for Kids* | $18.95 |
| _____ *Preschool Learning Activities* | $19.95 |
| _____ *Parents' Guide to Helping Kids Become "A" Students* | $11.95 |
| _____ *Divorced Dad's Handbook* | $12.95 |
| _____ *Expanding Your Child's Horizons* | $12.95 |
| _____ *Road School* | $14.95 |
| _____ *Parent's Guide to a Problem Child* | $11.95 |
| _____ *Multicultural Education Resource Guide* | $12.95 |
| _____ *Dragon-Slaying for Couples* | $14.95 |

Shipping Charges: $2.50 for first book. Add 50¢ for each additional book.
**Total charges for books:** _____
**Total shipping charges:** _____
**TOTAL ENCLOSED:** _____

Checks, money orders, and credit cards accepte
NAME:_____
ADDRESS:_____
CITY, STATE, ZIP:_____

FOR MAIL ORDERS, complete the followin

Please charge my _____ VISA _____ MasterCard
Card# _____
Expiration Date: _____
Signature: _____
Phone#: _____

**BLUE BIRD PUBLISHING**
**2266 S. Dobson #275**
**Mesa AZ 85202**
**(602) 831-6063**
**FAX (602) 831-1829**
**E-mail: bluebird@bluebird1.com**
**Web site: http://www.bluebird1.com**